PRAYING the GOSPELS
with MARTIN LUTHER

PRAYING THE GOSPELS WITH MARTIN LUTHER

PRAYING the GOSPELS with MARTIN LUTHER

Finding Freedom in Love

Paul W. Meier

MALCOLM CREEK
PUBLISHING
Benton, KY

PRAYING THE GOSPELS WITH MARTIN LUTHER

Copyright © 2012 by Paul W. Meier.

Published by Malcolm Creek Publishing,
Benton, KY 42025.
All rights reserved, including the right of reproduction in whole or in part in any form.

13-digit print edition ISBN: 978-0-9852850-0-5
10-digit print edition ISBN: 0-9852850-0-1

Cover Design by Mary C. Findley
Edited by Bethany F. Brengan.

Visit my website at http://www.prayingthegospels.com

Scripture quotations are taken from these sources:

THE HOLY BIBLE, NEW INTERNATIONAL VERSION®, NIV®
Copyright © 1973, 1978, 1984, 2011 by Biblica, Inc.™ Used by permission.
All rights reserved worldwide.

Scripture taken from the New King James Version. Copyright © 1982 by Thomas Nelson, Inc. Used by permission. All rights reserved.

NASB: Scripture taken from the NEW AMERICAN STANDARD BIBLE®, Copyright ©
1960,1962,1963,1968,1971,1972,1973,1975,1977,1995 by The Lockman Foundation. Used by permission.

NRSV: New Revised Standard Version Bible, copyright 1989, Division of Christian Education of the National Council of the Churches of Christ in the United States of America. Used by permission. All rights reserved.

Library of Congress PCN: 2012902796

To my wife, Barbara,

and the members of St. Matthew by the Lake Lutheran Church
Benton, KY

for giving me the opportunity to study
and share what I learned in my reading of the Church Postils.

Other books by Paul W. Meier

In Living Color: The Lord's Prayer

In Living Color: The Beatitudes

30 Day To Loving God With All Your Heart

Be the Light: Overcoming Evil with Good

Table of Contents:

Introduction		...3
Matthew 2:1–12	The Wise Men Meet the Christ Child	...8
Matthew 4:1–11	Jesus Tempted in the Wilderness	...12
Matthew 5:20–26	Jesus' Teaching Clarifies the Law	...16
Matthew 6:24–34	Do Not Worry about Tomorrow	...20
Matthew 7:15–23	People Are Known by Their Fruits	...24
Matthew 8:1–13	Jesus Cleanses a Leper, Heals a Centurion's Servant	...28
Matthew 8:23–27	Jesus Stills the Storm	...32
Matthew 9:1–8	Jesus Forgives and Heals a Paralytic	...36
Matthew 9:18–26	A Girl Restored to Life and a Woman Healed	...40
Matthew 11:2–11	John the Baptist Sends Messengers to Jesus	...44
Matthew 13:24–30	The Parable of Weeds among the Wheat	...48
Matthew 15:21–28	The Canaanite Woman's Faith	...52
Matthew 18:23–35	The Parable of the Unforgiving Servant	...56
Matthew 20:1–16	The Laborers in the Vineyard	...60
Matthew 21:1–9	Jesus' Entry into Jerusalem	...64
Matthew 22:1–14	The Parable of the Wedding Banquet	...68
Matthew 22:15–22	The Question about Paying Taxes	...72
Matthew 22:34–46	The Greatest Commandment	...76
Matthew 23:34–39	Woes to the Pharisees	...80
Matthew 24:15–28	The Great Tribulation	...84
Matthew 25:31–46	Separating the Sheep and Goats	...88
Mark 7:31–37	Jesus Heals a Man Deaf and Mute	...92
Mark 8:1–9	Jesus Feeds Four Thousand	...96
Mark 16:1–8	The Resurrection of Jesus	...100
Mark 16:14–20	Jesus Commissions the Disciples	...104
Luke 2:1–14	Jesus' Birth and Announcement to the Shepherds	...108
Luke 2:15–20	The Shepherds Visit Jesus	...112

Luke 2:33–40	Jesus is Brought to the Temple	…116
Luke 2:41–52	Twelve-Year-Old Jesus in the Temple	…120
Luke 5:1–11	Jesus Calls the First Disciples	…124
Luke 6:36–42	Teaching on Forgiveness and Judgment	…128
Luke 7:11–17	Jesus Raises the Widow's Son at Nain	…132
Luke 8:4–15	The Parable of the Sower	…136
Luke 10:23–37	The Parable of the Good Samaritan	…140
Luke 11:14–23	Jesus and Beelzebul	…144
Luke 14:1–11	Jesus Heals on the Sabbath and Teaches Humility	…148
Luke 14:16–24	The Parable of the Invitation to the Great Feast	…152
Luke 15:1–10	The Parable of the Lost Sheep and Lost Coin	…156
Luke 16:1–9	The Parable of the Shrewd Manager	…160
Luke 16:19–31	The Rich Man and Lazarus	…164
Luke 17:11–19	Jesus Cleanses Ten Lepers	…168
Luke 18:9–14	Parable of the Pharisee and Tax Collector	…172
Luke 18:31–43	A Blind Man Recognizes the Messiah	…176
Luke 19:41–48	Jesus Weeps over Jerusalem	…180
Luke 21:25–36	The Coming of the Son of Man	…184
Luke 24:13–35	The Walk to Emmaus	…188
Luke 24:36–47	The Ascension of Jesus	…192
John 1:1–14	Jesus is the Living Word	…196
John 1:19–28	The Testimony of John the Baptist	…200
John 2:1–11	The Wedding in Cana	…204
John 3:1–15	Nicodemus Visits Jesus	…208
John 3:16–21	God's Love for the World	…212
John 4:46–54	Jesus Heals the Official's Son	…216
John 6:1–15	Feeding the Five Thousand	…220
John 6:44–51	The Bread of Life	…224

John 8:46–59	Glorifying the Father instead of Abraham	...228
John 10:1–11	Jesus the Gatekeeper	...232
John 10:11–16	Jesus the Good Shepherd	...236
John 14:23–31	The Promise of the Holy Spirit	...240
John 15:26–16:4	Persecution for Following Christ	...244
John 16:5–15	The Work of the Spirit	...248
John 16:16–23	Sorrow Will Turn into Joy	...252
John 16:23–30	Jesus Mediates for Us	...256
John 20:19–31	Jesus Appears to His Disciples	...260
John 21:19–24	Jesus Redirects Peter's Concern	...264

A Prayer for Good Friday—How to Contemplate Christ's Sufferings ...268

A Prayer for Confession and the Lord's Supper ...272

Works Cited ...277

PRAYING THE GOSPELS WITH MARTIN LUTHER

* * *

"Therefore we conclude that all law, divine and human, treating of outward conduct, should not bind any further than love goes. Love is to be the interpreter of law."
(Vol. 5:161)

* * *

Introduction

*"Prayer is a very precious medicine,
one that helps and never fails."* Martin Luther
(Luther 1956, vol. 21)

The daily and diligent practice of prayer opened a portal for Martin Luther to hear the voice of God, especially as he meditated on Holy Scripture. For much of my life I thought, *There's not enough time to spend more than a few brief moments every day in prayer.* The only prayers I could manage were offered on the run.

Martin Luther held an opposite view of the importance of prayer. It's reported that he spent two hours in prayer and meditation every morning. If he anticipated a particularly stressful day, he spent an extra hour in prayer. People who pause to listen for the voice of God and who invite God to guide their efforts are people who end up moving mountains. They become God's instruments for change in the world.

I wondered, *What led Luther to attach such great value to prayer? Is this where he gained new understanding and found strength to stand up to twelve hundred years of tradition?* When a friend showed me a book of prayers (*Praying in the Wesleyan Spirit* by Paul Chilcote) designed to teach the themes in John Wesley's sermons, I thought, *I could do the same with Martin Luther's sermons in the Church Postil.* To write prayers arising from Luther's sermons on the gospels might be an efficient way of learning what he believed important for the people in the pews to understand. At the same time, this would encourage the practice of prayer.

Systematically, I began reading the sermons based on the gospel texts in the *Church Postil*, taking copious notes on each one. Sometimes there were two or three sermons for a text. Once I developed an overall feel for what Luther was emphasizing in the text, I began writing a prayer for each sermon text based on my notes and the biblical text.

What appealed to me in Luther's sermons was his focus on love as the determining factor in knowing and fulfilling God's will. He explained how to discern which laws in Scripture are viable and which ones are not to be followed. He preached that we can only show our love for God through loving our neighbor. And he left no doubt that salvation that comes through faith alone by the grace of God produces more good works for our neighbor than the church in Rome ever demanded of anyone.

Luther's sermons gave me a new sense of freedom—a new kind of power and confidence to be bold in my faith walk. I believe the concepts I share in the prayers of this book will give you that same freedom.

How to Use these Prayers

Allow yourself fifteen or twenty minutes to enter into a meaningful exchange during prayer. Just like it takes time to knead yeast into dough when making bread, you must allow Wisdom the time to knead the truth into your heart, mind, and soul.

Find a secluded place where you will have a minimum of interruptions. Sit in a comfortable position, take a few deep breaths, and release the tension from your shoulders, neck, arms, back, and legs. Be creative in your efforts to enter the inner room of your heart. Begin with a brief prayer asking the Holy Spirit to open your heart and guide your thoughts.

Each prayer in this book begins with a quotation from Luther's sermon on a gospel text. The number preceding the quotation refers to a corresponding paragraph number in that sermon on my website (http://www.prayingthegospels.com) or in John Lenker's 1983 edition of the *Sermons of Martin Luther*. The page number is listed after the volume number (e.g., Vol. 2:125) and will help you to find the quotation. When there are two or three sermons for one text, the page numbers are inserted into the online sermons at the place they appear in the print version.

Read the quotation slowly. Ask yourself, "How does this apply to my life today?"

The gospel text is printed next. Read it slowly. Let it be the foundation for your prayer.

Next, read the prayer slowly, one phrase at a time. Pause for reflection when something connects with your life experience. Can you see where a phrase connects to the Scripture text?

Give yourself permission to stay with a prayer phrase for as long as it speaks to you. Reflection is a powerful component of prayer that many people neglect. It's one of the central places from which the voice of God arises.

Each prayer concludes with a verse or two from a hymn written by Martin Luther. He believed God spoke to people through the Bible and hymnody was the people's response to God. Use the words of the hymn as a response to what you have heard in your prayer time.

* * *

You can search for a prayer based on a biblical story that interests you. You can identify a prayer according to a theme that touches your life. Or you can simply open the book and begin with any prayer. If you like to begin your weekday with a short devotion, use these prayers for the next three months.

If you know in advance which gospel text is planned in your congregation for a coming Sunday, you might select that prayer as a preparation for your worship. Pray it a day or two prior to Sunday and then another day or two after you worship. You may find the gospel connecting with events in your life when you stay with a prayer over this length of time. And you will undoubtedly hear a new Word after deeper meditation.

Small groups or Sunday school classes could use these prayers as a guide to discussing Scripture texts through the year.

The Church Postil

The word *postil* means "explanation." The *Church Postil* is a collection of Martin Luther's sermons, written and edited from 1520–1544. He wrote them for local clergy to use for preaching and teaching the meanings of Scripture texts. Many priests of that time were not skilled in biblical analysis. When they preached, they often read from the New Testament, or they would read a sermon from one of the more popular preachers of the day. John Nicholas Lenker, editor of the 1983 edition, said Luther considered his *Church Postil* to be the "best of all his books."

Themes repeated in Luther's sermons might surprise you. He emphasized good works and service to your neighbor. He frequently explained things he saw hidden in texts that went beyond the plain meanings. You might also find it appealing how the Word spoke personally to Luther. The Spirit guided him to apply the Scriptures to his own life. He connected the people and events in the Bible to the people in his time. When Luther meditated on Scripture, no time barrier existed between the first century and the sixteenth century.

* * *

The diversity of topics, the depth of his interpretations, and the underlying spiritual meanings explained in his sermons cannot be covered in the brevity of these prayers. My objective was not to condense his sermons point by point, but to highlight themes that spoke to me. I did not attempt to confirm nor conform to scholarly interpretation of Luther's works. I also modified Luther's terminology whenever it referred to the papacy, church councils, or specific doctrines and practices of the Roman Catholic Church in the sixteenth century. I want you to be able to apply these messages to the Christian Church in its diversity today.

A complete history of Martin Luther's *Church Postil* can be found in the editor's introduction to the *Sermons of Martin Luther*, published by Baker Books and edited by John Nicholas Lenker. Luther's sermons are in the public domain. If any of these prayers spark your interest to learn more about Luther's postils, you can find his sermons listed by Scripture text on my website: www.prayingthegospels.com.

Luther's Hymns

Martin Luther applied his talents beyond biblical translation and interpretation. He loved music and wanted to bring the gospel to people through the penetrating medium of song. Luther reasoned that within spiritual songs the Word of God and Christian doctrine could help people understand how to put their faith into practice in daily life. One of his primary goals was to repeat the message of the grace of God in Christ: Christ alone is our praise and our song. Many of Luther's hymns can be found online at
http://www.iclnet.org/pub/resources/text/wittenberg/wittenberg-hymnals.html.

Cover of the book: The picture on the cover is one of the caves at Qumran where the Dead Sea Scrolls were discovered. Martin Luther said we can find the gospel in both testaments, in the promise of the Messiah and then in the fulfillment of that promise. The image is a reminder that treasure can be found in unexpected places. I hope you find a treasure worth sharing with others as you meditate on these prayers.

* * *

96. "Reason and nature never proceed any farther than they can see and feel.... The light of nature and the light of grace cannot be friends. Nature wants to feel and be certain before she believes, grace believes before she perceives." (Vol. 1:362)

* * *

Matthew 2:1–12
The Wise Men Meet the Christ Child

In the time of King Herod, after Jesus was born in Bethlehem of Judea, wise men from the East came to Jerusalem, asking, "Where is the child who has been born king of the Jews? For we observed his star at its rising, and have come to pay him homage."

When King Herod heard this, he was frightened, and all Jerusalem with him; and calling together all the chief priests and scribes of the people, he inquired of them where the Messiah was to be born. They told him, "In Bethlehem of Judea; for so it has been written by the prophet: 'And you, Bethlehem, in the land of Judah, are by no means least among the rulers of Judah; for from you shall come a ruler who is to shepherd my people Israel.'" Then Herod secretly called for the wise men and learned from them the exact time when the star had appeared. Then he sent them to Bethlehem, saying, "Go and search diligently for the child; and when you have found him, bring me word so that I may also go and pay him homage.

When they had heard the king, they set out; and there, ahead of them, went the star that they had seen at its rising, until it stopped over the place where the child was. When they saw that the star had stopped, they were overwhelmed with joy. On entering the house, they saw the child with Mary his mother; and they knelt down and paid him homage. Then, opening their treasure chests, they offered him gifts of gold, frankincense, and myrrh. And having been warned in a dream not to return to Herod, they left for their own country by another road." (NRSV)

True Light of the World,

The Holy Scriptures shine their light on You, and You reveal the Almighty God. How could the wise men believe a child in a humble stable was a king unless You made this known to them? Teach me to discern the truth about You through the Scriptures. Help me to abandon human teachings that do not arise from the Word of God.

Lord, grant me new vision that I might see how religious leaders today imitate Herod. Some *say* they want to worship the Newborn King, but they create human ordinances and reliance on self-effort, which takes my eyes off the Christ Child. I want my life and worship to be for the Child alone. If ever I hold a position of leadership in the church, help me to avoid any sense of self-importance. And forgive me every time I fail.

When I imagine my failures could put an end to Your favor, guide me to Christ like the star guided the Magi to the Child in the manger. This light symbolizes the gospel that is preached, and it reveals the pure grace of God. Draw me, with all people, to the Child, that we might make Him our King. May the proclamation of the Word remain over Christ and go no further by adding requirements that go beyond trust in Him.

O Lord, You did not exalt Yourself over any man, woman, or child. You have blessed the secular professions over the priestly position because they encourage people to be of bodily benefit to each other. Assure me that helping my neighbor who is in need is of greater value to You than spiritual works and rituals.

Because it's difficult to change what I've been taught for so long, lead me to recognize that my work outside the church is as important as any sacred labor performed within the church. Give me joy in humbly fulfilling my responsibilities as a member of a Christian congregation. And open my eyes to see opportunities where I live and work to use my abilities for the benefit of others.

I know the good works I perform do not liberate me from the burden of sin. Yet guide me to the all-embracing peace Your forgiveness brings as I confess my sin and trust in Your grace.

I offer You the only thing that is mine to give You, my praise and thanksgiving. Everything else I possess has been Your gift to me. Thank You, Jesus. Amen.

1. Why, Herod, unrelenting foe,
   Doth the Lord's coming move thee so?
   He doth no earthly kingdom seek
   Who brings his kingdom to the meek.

2. Led by the star, the wise men find
   The Light that lightens all mankind;
   The threefold presents which they bring
   Declare him God, and Man, and King.
   (Luther 1884y)

* * *

24. "For whom the devil cannot overcome with poverty, want, need and misery, he attacks with riches, favor, honor, pleasure, power and the like, and contends on both sides against us; yea, 'he walketh about,' says St. Peter in 1 Pet 5:8, so that if he cannot overthrow us either with suffering or love, … he retires to a higher and different method and attacks us with error, blindness and a false understanding of the Scripture." (Vol. 2:145)

* * *

Matthew 4:1–11

Jesus Tempted in the Wilderness

Then Jesus was led by the Spirit into the desert to be tempted by the devil. After fasting forty days and forty nights, he was hungry. The tempter came to him and said, "If you are the Son of God, tell these stones to become bread." Jesus answered, "It is written: 'Man does not live on bread alone, but on every word that comes from the mouth of God.'"

Then the devil took him to the holy city and had him stand on the highest point of the temple. "If you are the Son of God," he said, "throw yourself down. For it is written: "He will command his angels concerning you, and they will lift you up in their hands, so that you will not strike your foot against a stone.'" Jesus answered him, "It is also written: 'Do not put the Lord your God to the test.'"

Again, the devil took him to a very high mountain and showed him all the kingdoms of the world and their splendor. "All this I will give you," he said, "if you will bow down and worship me." Jesus said to him, "Away from me, Satan! For it is written: 'Worship the Lord your God, and serve him only.'" Then the devil left him, and angels came and attended him. (NIV 1984)

Word of Life,

The benefit of fasting isn't always clear to me. Please help me understand how refraining from food can help me spiritually. If You think the practice of fasting might help bring the desires of my flesh under control, lead me to want to fast. If not, let me be thankful for the physical nourishment You are providing me.

I'm in such a hurry to advance in life and faith that I rush into wildernesses I create for myself. When I feel alone and unsatisfied with my life, keep me from inventing ways to compensate for my emptiness.

Give me wisdom and patience to let the Spirit lead me into places where my faith can be stretched. May the Word help me to turn the evil one away.

I am tempted to think You don't love me when my physical needs are at risk. I start falling for the world's promises that fortune, power, and fame will satisfy my desires. These are stones disguised as bread that cannot nourish my soul. Feed me the food that supports my spirit: the Word that assures me of Your desire to be my God.

The devil puts on a beautiful outward appearance, tempting me with pleasure and prosperity. Grant me power to resist craving glory for myself because then I think I deserve the blessings You have given me.

How weak I am, Lord. I can be attacked from so many sides. Can I ever trust You enough to be able to defend myself from so many temptations? Yes, because the Spirit has led me to these places and will teach me to trust in You. I pray You will send saintly messengers to tend to me when I am tempted to lose confidence in You.

Satan makes me think there are better ways to achieve a holy life than You have already provided. Trusting You and loving my neighbor appear too simple and boring. Lead me to walk the path that has long been provided instead of thinking dramatic deeds and leaps of faith are required. You, Jesus, are the Way. I want to trust in You and follow Your example. Amen.

7. Into temptation lead us not;
   And when the foe doth war and plot
   Against our souls on every hand,
   Then, armed with faith, O may we stand
   Against him as a valiant host,
   Through comfort of the Holy Ghost.

8. Deliver us from evil, Lord!
   The days are dark and foes abroad;
   Redeem us from eternal death;
   And when we yield our dying breath,
   Console us, grant us calm release,
   And take our souls to Thee in peace.
   (Luther 1884q)

* * *

7. "Now, this is the sum of the law: You are to be kind, amiable and benignant in heart, word and deed; and even though they take your life, still you are to suffer all in love, and render thanks to your Lord.... Christ lived up to this; do the same, and you are a good Christian." (Vol. 4:182)

* * *

Prayer for Matthew 5:20–26
Jesus' Teaching Clarifies the Law

[Jesus said] "For I tell you, unless your righteousness exceeds that of the scribes and Pharisees, you will never enter the kingdom of heaven.

"You have heard that it was said to those of ancient times, 'You shall not murder'; and 'whoever murders shall be liable to judgment.' But I say to you that if you are angry with a brother or sister, you will be liable to judgment; and if you insult a brother or sister, you will be liable to the council; and if you say, 'You fool,' you will be liable to the hell of fire.

"So when you are offering your gift at the altar, if you remember that your brother or sister has something against you, leave your gift there before the altar and go; first be reconciled to your brother or sister, and then come and offer your gift. Come to terms quickly with your accuser while you are on the way to court with him, or your accuser may hand you over to the judge, and the judge to the guard, and you will be thrown into prison. Truly I tell you, you will never get out until you have paid the last penny." (NRSV)

Judge of my Heart,

Even if I have in-depth knowledge of Scripture and outward obedience to the law, this does not render me exempt from sin. If Your kingdom is open only to those who harbor no anger, malice, or vengeance in their heart, I'm doomed.

How is it possible for me to avoid anger? Can You not see I'm only human? Yes. You do see me. You see directly into my heart, and You know when anger and hatred lie beneath my acts of kindness or obedience. I confess my failure to act out of love in all I do. Please let compassion be the motivation that leads me to live the way You lived.

I'm weary of religious leaders who rationalize rejecting those who do not worship rules invented by human institutions. I don't understand how they think they are serving God when sin is used to defeat sin. I pray for leaders who use the letter of the law to advance their own agendas. Soften their hearts. Teach them what You mean by justice. Help all to realize that the roots of obedience to the law run so deep that they reveal what is in a person's heart. Comfort and bring healing quickly to those who have been hurt because of someone's inflexibility concerning the law.

Christ, help me to be kind and amiable when anyone tries to harm me. To do this will confirm that I have been born from above. Rise up in me so that I can suffer any hurt in love. Remove any temptation to kill from my heart or with my tongue and any temptation to withhold aid that could help a person who has hurt me. Then let me give thanks that You have worked through me. Change me and make me an example of Your perfection.

You said You want me to be reconciled to my neighbor before offering my time, talents, or possessions. Instill within me the understanding that love is the gift You desire above all things, and without love for my neighbor, there is no love for You.

You have given us civil and religious courts to administer justice that does not exceed the crime committed. Guide our judges and courts, religious and civil alike, to be wise and prudent in their decisions, giving out sentences appropriate for the bodily and spiritual welfare of every person.

My Lord Jesus, You know the difficulty I face in trying to follow Your will perfectly. I cannot do this without You. Comfort and assure me of our heavenly Father's forgiving nature and lead me to rely on Your cleansing righteousness instead of my worthiness. When I fail, renew me in my efforts to exercise greater love so that I please You. Amen.

1. The mouth of fools doth God confess,
   But while their lips draw nigh Him
   Their heart is full of wickedness,
   And all their deeds deny Him.
   Corrupt are they, and every one
   Abominable deeds hath done;
   There is not one well-doer.
   (Luther 1884o)

* * *

16. "The sum of all is, it is God's will that we serve not gold and riches, and that we be not overanxious for our life; but that we labor and commend our anxiety to him. Whoever possesses riches is lord of the riches. Whoever serves them is their slave and does not possess them, but they possess him; for he [cannot] make use of them when he desires, and cannot serve others with them; yea, he is not bold enough to dare to touch it." (Vol. 5:109)

* * *

Prayer for Matthew 6:24–34
Do Not Worry about Tomorrow

[Jesus said], "No one can serve two masters; for either he will hate the one and love the other, or else he will be loyal to the one and despise the other. You cannot serve God and mammon.

Therefore I say to you, do not worry about your life, what you will eat or what you will drink; nor about your body, what you will put on. Is not life more than food and the body more than clothing? Look at the birds of the air, for they neither sow nor reap nor gather into barns; yet your heavenly Father feeds them. Are you not of more value than they? Which of you by worrying can add one cubit to his stature?

"So why do you worry about clothing? Consider the lilies of the field, how they grow: they neither toil nor spin; and yet I say to you that even Solomon in all his glory was not arrayed like one of these. Now if God so clothes the grass of the field, which today is, and tomorrow is thrown into the oven, will He not much more clothe you, O you of little faith?

"Therefore do not worry, saying, 'What shall we eat?' or 'What shall we drink?' or 'What shall we wear?' For after all these things the Gentiles seek. For your heavenly Father knows that you need all these things. But seek first the kingdom of God and His righteousness, and all these things shall be added to you. Therefore do not worry about tomorrow, for tomorrow will worry about its own things. Sufficient for the day is its own trouble. (NKJV)

Source and Provider of All That is Good,

Your Word comforts me and assures me that the Almighty God is like a loving Father who provides for my essential needs. My problem is that I want more than I need.

Forgive me when I think I deserve as much as those for whom money and possessions are gods. This only fosters anxiety and a lack of peace. Teach me to appreciate everything You provide.

When I am able to give things away, they serve me, and if I can't give possessions away when others need help, they rule over me. I don't want material belongings to govern me. I want to trust that You will provide for my needs as I allow You to reign in my life.

Serving two masters is like having two presidents or two kings in the same territory. They have conflicting interests and they become enemies of each other. Help me recognize that what You offer is to be prized far above gold which cannot comfort or clothing that wears out. I want to cherish You more than the gifts You give to me.

Sometimes I worry that I will lose the possessions I have worked so hard to acquire. Fear tells me I won't ever have enough to support myself. Why haven't I learned from what You taught, that the birds of the air or flowers in the field don't worry about such things? Help me to see that what I do today to help myself and others is more useful than fearing what might or might not happen tomorrow.

If what I do for others is not done cheerfully, why do I think these efforts please You? I don't enjoy gifts when I know they haven't been given willingly. I seek a heart and a will that loves You, trusts You, and recognizes You are my greatest treasure. Guide me, Lord, to put Your Word and teachings into practice. I can't say I follow You if I don't do as You have taught. You have the words that lead to true life.

I can't change the past. I can't control or predict the future. I ask for wisdom and courage to choose You as Lord of my life, trusting You will direct my ways. Amen.

1. We all believe in one true God,
    Maker of the earth and heaven,
    The Father who to us the power
    To become his sons hath given.
    He will us at all times nourish,
    Soul and body, guard us, guide us,
    'Mid all harms will keep and cherish,
    That no ill shall ever betide us.
    He watches o'er us day and night;
    All things are governed by his might.
    (Luther 1884x)

* * *

8. "Then they began to say: *'Yes, but how can we know what is God's Word, and what is right or wrong? We must learn this from the Pope and the councils.'* Very well then, let them conclude and say what they please, yet I will reply, you cannot put your confidence in that nor thus satisfy your conscience, for you must determine this matter yourself, for your very life depends upon it. Therefore God must speak to your heart: This is God's Word; otherwise you are undecided." (Vol. 4:234-290)

* * *

Prayer for Matthew 7:15–23
People Are Known by Their Fruits

[Jesus said] "Beware of false prophets, who come to you in sheep's clothing but inwardly are ravenous wolves. You will know them by their fruits. Are grapes gathered from thorns, or figs from thistles? In the same way, every good tree bears good fruit, but the bad tree bears bad fruit. A good tree cannot bear bad fruit, nor can a bad tree bear good fruit. Every tree that does not bear good fruit is cut down and thrown into the fire. Thus you will know them by their fruits.

"Not everyone who says to me, 'Lord, Lord,' will enter the kingdom of heaven, but only the one who does the will of my Father in heaven. On that day many will say to me, 'Lord, Lord, did we not prophesy in your name, and cast out demons in your name, and do many deeds of power in your name?' Then I will declare to them, 'I never knew you; go away from me, you evildoers.'" (NRSV)

Source of Goodness and Truth,

You summarized all of Christianity at the end of Your teaching on the mount by saying I should treat others the way I want to be treated. Let me keep this as the foundation of my actions, O Christ. Give me wisdom to filter out what others insist of me that is not from Your Word.

Some preachers think I should believe everything they say, but You have given me a brain, and I alone am responsible for what I accept as truth. After all, it's my soul that's at stake. With so many people confidently declaring their version of truth, help me to listen only to You, the Word that speaks to my heart.

Jesus, Your teaching is my guide. Guard me from thinking I must follow extra instructions invented by people. When people oppose me, let me stand firmly on the Word You give me in Scripture.

Wolves cover themselves with Scripture and it's hard to tell who's right and who's wrong. Teach me that I can judge good teaching from bad teaching through careful observation of a person's actions: Do they exhibit peace, joy, love, patience, mercy, and self-control? Let me recognize as false teachers those who show anger, cause division, or create conflict.

Help me to never to lead anyone astray by using unkind words or actions. I want to make the power of Your truth known through works of love that benefit my neighbor, the needy, my enemies, and sinners. Open the minds of those who have not understood You to discover joy when You reveal Yourself to them.

Guide my actions so my light will shine and display You as the power working in me. You have saved me. I believe that nothing more is required beyond trusting that my sin is forgiven and removed from Your sight. Let Your revelation of this truth to me spawn a depth of love for You that results in works of kindness for my neighbor. Amen.

6. Thus by the power of grace they were
   True priests of God's own making,
   Who offered up themselves e'en there,
   Christ's holy orders taking;
   Dead to the world, they cast aside
   Hypocrisy's sour leaven,
   That penitent and justified
   They might go clean to heaven,
   And leave all monkish follies.
   (Luther 1884e)

* * *

2. "This is true faith, a living confidence in the goodness of God. The heart that does this, has true faith; the heart that does it not, has not true faith; as they do who keep not the goodness of God and that alone in sight, but first look around for their own good works, in order to be worthy of God's grace and to merit it. These never become bold to call upon God earnestly or to draw near to him." (Vol. 2:72)

* * *

Prayer for Matthew 8:1–13
Jesus Cleanses a Leper, Heals a Centurion's Servant

When Jesus came down from the mountain, large crowds followed Him. And a leper came to Him and bowed down before Him, and said, "Lord, if You are willing, You can make me clean." Jesus stretched out His hand and touched him, saying, "I am willing; be cleansed." And immediately his leprosy was cleansed. And Jesus said to him, "See that you tell no one; but go, show yourself to the priest and present the offering that Moses commanded, as a testimony to them."

And when Jesus entered Capernaum, a centurion came to Him, imploring Him, and saying, "Lord, my servant is lying paralyzed at home, fearfully tormented." Jesus said to him, "I will come and heal him." But the centurion said, "Lord, I am not worthy for You to come under my roof, but just say the word, and my servant will be healed. For I also am a man under authority, with soldiers under me; and I say to this one, 'Go!' and he goes, and to another, 'Come!' and he comes, and to my slave, 'Do this!' and he does it."

Now when Jesus heard this, He marveled and said to those who were following, "Truly I say to you, I have not found such great faith with anyone in Israel. I say to you that many will come from east and west, and recline at the table with Abraham, Isaac and Jacob in the kingdom of heaven; but the sons of the kingdom will be cast out into the outer darkness; in that place there will be weeping and gnashing of teeth."

And Jesus said to the centurion, "Go; it shall be done for you as you have believed." And the servant was healed that very moment. (NASB)

Healer of my Soul,

Like the leper, I have heard of Your goodness, Your kindness, and Your ability to heal. May I be as bold as he was in seeking Your help so I may be cleansed of unrighteous actions. I offer nothing to suggest I deserve Your restoring touch. Assure me that nothing is required to make myself worthy of Your attention, and grant me complete confidence in Your mercy and power.

You are love, O Christ. Render me a servant who does not seek reward or honor for myself. Cleanse my motives so that when I help others, You are the one who is glorified.

Unlike the leper, the centurion was not part of the religious tradition and doctrines of the patriarchs and prophets. Yet You didn't hesitate to help him. Teach me to respond gladly when given the chance to help those I don't think of as Your chosen people.

Although being in authority over others can bring benefits, it also carries a great responsibility: the well-being and care of those under my supervision. Help me to care for them well.

You helped this man who was obviously not poor. Let me, in faith, gladly receive Your abundance and then offer these blessings to others so they can experience Your goodness too. Fill my heart with love, that I may consider it a privilege to share what I have received with my neighbor.

Trust in You is everything. You showed that sometimes You *do* heal through the faith of others. Hear my prayers for those I lift up to You, that they might learn to trust in Your goodness and mercy for themselves.

Lord, some people tell me that Bible study and religious practices are required to increase my faith, yet here is a man outside the religious tradition who possessed faith in You greater than those within the tradition. Guide me so that I don't rely on intellectual or ritual efforts when faith comes as a gift from You. I ask only for a simple faith, like a child, for Your kingdom belongs to those who trust in Your goodness. Amen.

3. 'Tis Christ our God, who far on high
   Had heard your sad and bitter cry;
   Himself will your salvation be,
   Himself from sin will make you free.

4. He brings those blessings long ago
   Prepared by God for all below;
   That in his heavenly kingdom blest
   You may with us forever rest.
   (Luther 1884f)

* * *

14. Thus it is ordained that the Word of God has no master nor judge, no protector or patron can be given it besides God himself. It is his Word. Therefore, as he left it go forth without any merit or counsel of men, so will he himself without any human help and strength administer and defend it. And whoever seeks protection and comfort in these things among men, will both fall and fail, and be forsaken by both God and man. (Vol. 2:98)

* * *

Prayer for Matthew 8:23–27
Jesus Stills the Storm

And when he got into the boat, his disciples followed him. A windstorm arose on the sea, so great that the boat was being swamped by the waves; but he was asleep. And they went and woke him up, saying, "Lord, save us! We are perishing!" And he said to them, "Why are you afraid, you of little faith?" Then he got up and rebuked the winds and the sea; and there was a dead calm. They were amazed, saying, "What sort of man is this, that even the winds and the sea obey him?" (NRSV)

Prince of Peace,

It's easy for me to think I trust in You when the seas of life are calm and peaceful. But being a Christian does not mean I'm safe from distressing events. There will be struggles, tears, and wounds. Give me confidence in Your presence to help me overcome circumstances that change quickly and often. Be the rock on which I stay grounded.

The world continually rises up against Christendom and its disciples. All who oppose the preaching of Christ alone, especially those Christians who preach the Law, crash against us like the wind and the waves. Allow me to find consolation in the outrage of law advocates who inflate their importance, including the saintly, the learned, and the wise. When I see they are ruffled because I point to You alone, assure me this is proof that I am doing Your will.

The Word needs no guard or protector other than God, the Author. Help me to simply do what Scripture teaches, rather than act as its defender. Guide me to focus my efforts on following what You taught, O Christ, which is to love my neighbor.

You always hear when I cry for help. In the same way, open my ears to hear the cries of others when storms in life assault them. Compel me to offer help, not because they have done anything to deserve it, but because You have poured Your love into me. Throughout Your life, You provided assistance to people in need without demanding payment. You acted only to bring glory to God. Lead me to follow Your example of helping without expecting to be rewarded.

You permit me to worry about things until I discover that I have no power to control them and I finally turn to You. All things depend on Your power and grace. Give me wisdom to see the futility of my efforts when I try to manage what is beyond my control.

Your wisdom is beyond comprehension. Even though I have heard how trials and persecution have spread Your Word and kingdom and given it strength, when I face them, I fear being weakened by them. At the same time, periods of peace, ease, and luxury lull me to inaction and I fail to share Your favor with others. Assist me in understanding how trials help me to grow.

As I face tomorrow, if difficult times bear down on me, let me be secure in knowing I will be surrounded by Your presence, Your wisdom, and power. Amen.

3. Though earth all full of devils were,
   Wide roaring to devour us;
   Yet fear we no such grievous fear,
   They shall not overpower us.
   This world's prince may still
   Scowl fierce as he will,
   He can harm us none,
   He's judged; the deed is done;
   One little word can fell him.
   (Luther 1884s)

* * *

4. Therefore, if the kingdom of Christ is to grow, we must keep out of it with the law, and not be busy with works; for it is not in harmony with it to say: Go out and run hither and thither and atone for your sins; you must observe and do this and that, if you will be free from sin; but directly, without any work and law, out of pure grace, your sins are forgiven. Therefore, it is beyond the sphere of the kingdom of Christ to urge the people with the law. (Vol. 5:198–199)

* * *

Prayer for Matthew 9:1–8
Jesus Forgives and Heals a Paralytic

Jesus stepped into a boat, crossed over and came to his own town. Some men brought to him a paralytic, lying on a mat. When Jesus saw their faith, he said to the paralytic, "Take heart, son; your sins are forgiven."

At this, some of the teachers of the law said to themselves, "This fellow is blaspheming!"

Knowing their thoughts, Jesus said, "Why do you entertain evil thoughts in your hearts? Which is easier: to say, 'Your sins are forgiven,' or to say, 'Get up and walk'? But so that you may know that the Son of Man has authority on earth to forgive sins..." Then he said to the paralytic, "Get up, take your mat and go home." And the man got up and went home. When the crowd saw this, they were filled with awe; and they praised God, who had given such authority to men. (NIV, 1984)

Comfort of my Soul,

I want You to reign in me. I want Your kingdom to come. Your actions to heal the paralytic placed no requirements on him, not even obedience to the Law. Teach me how comfort and forgiveness of sins are the actions that draw people to You. In the power of the Holy Spirit, guide me to comprehend Your grace so it can lead me to good works.

Before I could walk in a way that was pleasing to You, You said, "Your sins are forgiven." How sweet it is to hear this good news. These words open my awareness to sin as a part of my life. I would need no forgiveness if I were without sin. Hear my confession. Let me feel the sweet comfort of Your grace as I listen to Your words of forgiveness again and again.

If I could follow the law, I would avoid the consequences of disobedience and enjoy Your gifts. Yet merely following the law does not make me a Christian. Lead me to a godliness that comes only as a gift in Christ. I want to trust in Your grace and forgiveness; for in You alone, I am protected, and no longer subject to the wrath of God.

You became my substitute. Your suffering and death satisfied all punishment for my sins. Let the joy of this knowledge stimulate me to go out and bless my neighbors who are in need. Give me wisdom to see that many people require their physical needs be met before they can listen to You for the healing of their souls. Tearing down people with the law cannot free them from sin. Help me to build up the consciences of others through the comfort of forgiveness.

Only You can give power to trust that walking in the will of God is a better path. Increase my desire to hear the Word of forgiveness in its public proclamation so the Holy Spirit can teach me the depths of Your grace and lead me to greater works of faith.

You have provided wonderful signs of Your forgiveness in baptism and Holy Communion. Some churches baptize infants. Yet infants can't confess their sins and they don't have any faith of their own. Give me a simple trust that You accept the prayers of faith from those who bring them to you —parents, sponsors, and the church. You are the One who makes a person whole by giving the child a faith of its own. Amen.

2. Jesus, Saviour with us stay,
   Nor suffer us to perish;
   All our sins O take away,
   Us dying, cheer and cherish.
   From the power of hell defend;
   This grace to us be granted:—
   Upon thee to be planted,
   In heartfelt faith undaunted,
   Trusting thee unto the end;
   With saints of every nation,
   Escaping hell's temptation,
   Kept by the Lord's salvation.
   Amen! Amen! Answer send!
   So sing we all Hallelujah!
    (Luther 1884g)

* * *

4. For this reason the Lord is pictured to us in today's Gospel, mingling among the people, drawing all the world unto himself by his friendliness and comforting doctrine so that they may cling to him with their hearts, depend upon his goodness, and hope to receive from him both spiritual and temporal treasures. Nor do you see him take anything from those he heals and helps; yea, he receives nothing from them but scorn and mockery, as we shall hear. (Vol. 5:328–343)

* * *

Prayer for Matthew 9:18–26
A Girl Restored to Life and a Woman Healed

While [Jesus] was saying these things to them, suddenly a leader of the synagogue came in and knelt before him, saying, "My daughter has just died; but come and lay your hand on her, and she will live." And Jesus got up and followed him, with his disciples.

Then suddenly a woman who had been suffering from hemorrhages for twelve years came up behind him and touched the fringe of his cloak, for she said to herself, "If I only touch his cloak, I will be made well." Jesus turned, and seeing her he said, "Take heart, daughter; your faith has made you well." And instantly the woman was made well.

When Jesus came to the leader's house and saw the flute-players and the crowd making a commotion, he said, "Go away; for the girl is not dead but sleeping." And they laughed at him. But when the crowd had been put outside, he went in and took her by the hand, and the girl got up. And the report of this spread throughout that district.
(NRSV)

Healer and Friend,

You are the gospel. You are the good news. Lead me to understand that the gospel has no rules or requirements attached to You. All other writings that go beyond declaring You as Savior are written to be instructive and are presented for Your sake.

The good news is declared when people share how You have touched their lives in wonderful ways. I am in awe of Your overflowing goodness and grace. You always give without requiring anything in return. I am humbled and thankful.

Give me wisdom and courage to reject the teachings of people who insist we follow the commandments and church laws in order to be forgiven. God forgives my sins only through Divine grace. In gratitude, stir me to pour out kindness to others.

O Christ, be my Savior, not my judge any longer. All who come to You receive help whether for healing, teaching, or peace in their life. Bless me with the understanding that all my prayers are heard and answered. Even though I may take for granted the privilege of an audience with You, lead me to ask boldly that I may receive of Your goodness and power.

Help me to comprehend, dear Lord, that the true preparation for receiving Your grace is that I feel my need of it. Heal me every time I reach for You through the Word and sacrament, believing that I have touched the fringe of Your cloak. Relieve me of the guilt that drains my soul. Strengthen my weak faith and warm my cold heart, so that love may flow from me to my neighbor.

I am a Christian, not because I claim to be one, but because I trust in You and find comfort in You. Like the synagogue leader, draw me to You even when circumstances appear impossible to change because they go beyond all logic and reason. I will trust You have the power to help.

Guide me to see death in the way You see it, as only sleep. Comfort me when I think otherwise, and assure me that You hold the lives of those who have died in rest that is sweet and brief until You come and awaken Your people.

Holy and Anointed One, You do not demand payment in return for the good gifts You offer. May Your comfort and blessing draw the best fruit from me. And lead me to give without thinking others should return the kindnesses I offer. Amen.

1. In peace and joy I now depart,
    At God's disposing;
    For full of comfort is my heart,
    Soft reposing.
    So the Lord hath promis'd me,
    And death is but a slumber.

2. 'Tis Christ that wrought this work for me,
    The faithful Saviour;
    Whom thou hast made mine eyes to see
    By thy favor.
    In him I behold my life,
    My help in need and dying.
    (Luther 1884i)

* * *

56. But know that to serve God is nothing else than to serve your neighbor and do good to him in love, be it a child, wife, servant, enemy, friend.... O, Lord God, how do we fools live in this world, neglecting to do such works, though in all parts of the world we find the needy, on whom we could bestow our good works; but no one looks after them nor cares for them. But look to your own life. If you do not find yourself among the needy and the poor, where the Gospel shows us Christ, then you may know that your faith is not right, and that you have not yet tasted of Christ's benevolence and work for you. (Vol. 1:111)

* * *

Prayer for Matthew 11:2–11
John the Baptist Sends Messengers to Jesus

And when John had heard in prison about the works of Christ, he sent two of his disciples and said to Him, "Are You the Coming One, or do we look for another?"

Jesus answered and said to them, "Go and tell John the things which you hear and see: The blind see and the lame walk; the lepers are cleansed and the deaf hear; the dead are raised up and the poor have the gospel preached to them. And blessed is he who is not offended because of Me."

As they departed, Jesus began to say to the multitudes concerning John: "What did you go out into the wilderness to see? A reed shaken by the wind? But what did you go out to see? A man clothed in soft garments? Indeed, those who wear soft clothing are in kings' houses. But what did you go out to see? A prophet? Yes, I say to you, and more than a prophet. For this is he of whom it is written:

'Behold, I send My messenger before Your face,
Who will prepare Your way before You.'

"Assuredly, I say to you, among those born of women there has not risen one greater than John the Baptist; but he who is least in the kingdom of heaven is greater than he." (NKJV)

Merciful Christ,

No earthly prophet, priest, or leader can guide me like You, my Lord Jesus Christ. Teach me. Lead me to build my faith on You and not the person delivering the message, no matter how pious and dynamic he may be. You are my Lord and Savior. May You increase in me while all messengers decrease.

O Christ, You pointed to Your works to encourage people to believe in You. Help me see that whenever the eyes of the blind open, the deaf hear, the lame walk, the hurting are comforted, the prisoners are freed, and the gospel is preached, You are there. Stir me to follow

Your compassionate example. Let my good works testify that You are within me.

I know Your Law is good. It teaches me the right way to live. Grant me Your grace to follow appropriate laws that serve love because it pleases You rather than following them for the reward of heaven or, as many teach, to escape from hell.

Sometimes I think I have the power to do something for You. It inflates my ego to think You need anything from me. It's always the other way around. I can do nothing for You except rejoice in the gospel's promise of grace and forgiveness in You. Let this understanding fill me with a peace I've never known before.

I fool myself by thinking religious forms and practices honor You when my neighbor lies neglected and in great need. Just as You come to me in my need, grant me boldness to put my faith into action by helping those who cannot help themselves.

In my human condition, I am blind to the needs of others. I am unable to walk the straight and narrow. I am imprisoned by fear, dead in my sins, and spiritually poor. I am one of the weak that You came to save. Help me to recognize that You rescue, not the self-sufficient, but those who see their need for You. Give me greater joy and security in understanding Your mercy than any amount of wealth or power the world could provide.

Merciful Savior, inspire me to demonstrate my love for God as I consent to Your work through me. I will point to You as the source of all healing. Amen.

1. Come, God Creator, Holy Ghost,
　　And visit thou these souls of men;
　　Fill them with graces, as thou dost,
　　Thy creatures make pure again.

3. Our minds illumine and refresh,
　　Deep in our hearts let love burn bright;
　　Thou know'st the weakness of our flesh;
　　And strengthen us with Thy might.
　　(Luther 1884c)

* * *

4. Again this Gospel teaches how we should conduct ourselves toward heretics and false teachers. We are not to uproot nor destroy them. Here he says publicly let both grow together. We have to do here with God's Word alone; for in this matter he who errs today may find the truth tomorrow. Who knows when the Word of God may touch his heart? (Vol. 2:102)

* * *

Prayer for Matthew 13:24–30
The Parable of Weeds among the Wheat

[Jesus] put before them another parable: "The kingdom of heaven may be compared to someone who sowed good seed in his field; but while everybody was asleep, an enemy came and sowed weeds among the wheat, and then went away. So when the plants came up and bore grain, then the weeds appeared as well. And the slaves of the householder came and said to him, 'Master, did you not sow good seed in your field? Where, then, did these weeds come from?' He answered, 'An enemy has done this.' The slaves said to him, 'Then do you want us to go and gather them?' But he replied, 'No; for in gathering the weeds you would uproot the wheat along with them. Let both of them grow together until the harvest; and at harvest time I will tell the reapers, Collect the weeds first and bind them in bundles to be burned, but gather the wheat into my barn.'" (NRSV)

Sower of Good Seed,

You have placed true Christians in the field of the world. Give me insight to see that Satan craftily sows both false Christians and heretics among us. They think by their works and doctrines they advance themselves in Your sight. Grant us grace to live together without destroying one another.

Forgive me when I think I can tell the difference between true Christians and false Christians simply by looking at their outward appearances. Judging them is not my task. Who am I to imagine that I can see inside another person's heart? Guide me to focus my efforts on sharing Your Word and bearing good fruit. And give me hope that those who don't understand Your grace correctly today may hear and accept the truth tomorrow.

As Your disciple, You have not directed me to uproot or destroy the heretics, false Christians, and unbelievers in our midst. No one learns to trust in You by force, threat, or penalty. That's not good news. Sometimes good people are lost to the faith because they see wrong actions done in God's name.

Forgive me, O Christ, for thinking I do God a service by harming or condemning anyone who does not believe as I do. Grant me honesty to grasp that when any individual or organized body advocates the ruin of those who disagree with it, it is a false teacher.

Bless me with wisdom that recognizes Your Word alone possesses the power to change people. Support me as I try to live out my faith in ways that make the Word visible. This is how others will be drawn to You.

Only You are able to establish true children of the kingdom. Protect me from the influence of the evil one. Help me discern which teachers I should believe by observing the truth shown in their fruit and good works. Then let me concentrate on bearing fruit of my own.

Build up patience in me as I live among false Christians and unbelievers. And give me persistence to keep working on myself, so that I will grow in trust and love for You, commending everyone else to Your care. Amen.

2. With frauds which they themselves invent
   Thy truth they have confounded;
   Their hearts are not with one consent
   On thy pure doctrine grounded;
   And, whilst they gleam with outward show,
   They lead Thy people to and fro,
   In error's maze astounded.

3. God surely will uproot all those
   With vain deceits who store us,
   With haughty tongue who God oppose,
   And say, "Who'll stand before us?
   By right or might we will prevail;
   What we determine cannot fail,
   For who can lord it o'er us?"
   (Luther 1884k)

* * *

11. Now whoever understands here the actions of this poor woman and catches God in his own judgment, and says: Lord, it is true, I am a sinner and not worthy of thy grace; but still thou hast promised sinners forgiveness, and thou art come not to call the righteous, but, as St. Paul says in I Tim 1, 15, "to save sinners." Behold, then must God according to his own judgment have mercy upon us. (Vol. 2:153)

* * *

Prayer for Matthew 15:21–28
The Canaanite Woman's Faith

Jesus went away from there, and withdrew into the district of Tyre and Sidon. And a Canaanite woman from that region came out and began to cry out, saying, "Have mercy on me, Lord, Son of David; my daughter is cruelly demon-possessed." But He did not answer her a word. And His disciples came and implored Him, saying, "Send her away, because she keeps shouting at us." But He answered and said, "I was sent only to the lost sheep of the house of Israel." But she came and began to bow down before Him, saying, "Lord, help me!" And He answered and said, "It is not good to take the children's bread and throw it to the dogs." But she said, "Yes, Lord; but even the dogs feed on the crumbs which fall from their masters' table." Then Jesus said to her, "O woman, your faith is great; it shall be done for you as you wish." And her daughter was healed at once.
(NASB)

Compassionate Physician,

I have heard how You healed the sick and cast demons from the lives of others. You do this even today. That's why I come to You. Through their witness and Your Word, grant me confidence in Your goodness and power to heal. Validate my trust in this good news that I may always run to You in my need.

I get discouraged quickly when my prayers seem to fall on deaf ears. I shouldn't expect You to act as soon as I snap my fingers. Forgive my impatience and disrespect. Many have seen and testify to your kindness. I want to believe You will help everyone who is in need.

Therefore, I will continue to bring my prayers to You. Strengthen my trust in You so that fear and doubt do not overtake me. In my heart, I know You hear me. Encourage me in the silence to hope in Your power to heal. I will wait in increasing expectancy for Your help.

I truly appreciate the prayers of other Christians on my behalf. They are Your disciples. They, too, must get frustrated when results don't come quickly. Please help us all to persist and not give up praying for people in need, even when answers don't come soon.

I know the Bible gives the impression that You turn away from people who don't turn their lives over to You. But I won't let those words stop me. I will trust the testimony of those who have seen your goodness and power for themselves. Satisfy my hope that You will heal my loved ones even when they have no faith of their own.

I may not feel that I am as important as people who follow You closely, but I am Your creation and I believe in Your goodness and power. I am what I am and I don't ask for anything more than a poor creature is entitled to from Your vast storehouse. Expel the demon from my own soul, and from the souls of those I love. You have promised forgiveness to sinners, and I claim that promise.

In the midst of all my feelings of rejection, assure me of my place as one of Your chosen people. Prove that my trust in Your goodness is justified. And thank You that Your lovingkindness is so great. Amen.

5. Not one he will nor can forsake
   Who him his confidence doth make:
   Let all his wiles the tempter try,
   You may his utmost powers defy.

6. You must prevail at last, for ye
   Are now become God's family:
   To God forever give ye praise,
   Patient and cheerful all your days.
   (Luther 1884w)

* * *

4. We have often said that the Gospel or kingdom of God is nothing else than a state or government, in which there is nothing but forgiveness of sins. And wherever there is a state or government in which sins are not forgiven, no Gospel or kingdom of God is found there.... In the kingdom of God, where God rules with the Gospel, there is no demand for right and dues, but all is pure forgiveness, pardon and giving, no anger, no punishment, but all is pure brotherly service and kindness. (Vol. 5:280–281)

* * *

Prayer for Matthew 18:23–35
The Parable of the Unforgiving Servant

[Jesus said] *"For this reason the kingdom of heaven may be compared to a king who wished to settle accounts with his slaves. When he began the reckoning, one who owed him ten thousand talents was brought to him; and, as he could not pay, his lord ordered him to be sold, together with his wife and children and all his possessions, and payment to be made. So the slave fell on his knees before him, saying, 'Have patience with me, and I will pay you everything.' And out of pity for him, the lord of that slave released him and forgave him the debt. But that same slave, as he went out, came upon one of his fellow slaves who owed him a hundred denarii; and seizing him by the throat, he said, 'Pay what you owe.' Then his fellow slave fell down and pleaded with him, 'Have patience with me, and I will pay you.' But he refused; then he went and threw him into prison until he would pay the debt. When his fellow slaves saw what had happened, they were greatly distressed, and they went and reported to their lord all that had taken place. Then his lord summoned him and said to him, 'You wicked slave! I forgave you all that debt because you pleaded with me. Should you not have had mercy on your fellow slave, as I had mercy on you?' And in anger his lord handed him over to be tortured until he would pay his entire debt. So my heavenly Father will also do to every one of you, if you do not forgive your brother or sister from your heart."* (NRSV)

Author of Forgiveness,

You see things so differently from the way the world sees them. Give me insight, dear Jesus. I want to understand how I can be expected to let go of unloving actions done to me over and over. Yet You have forgiven me so much and so many times for the same sin. I want to be able to forgive my neighbor the way you have forgiven me.

Open my heart to grasp that In Your kingdom there is nothing but forgiveness of sin, pardon, and giving. There is no anger, no punishment, pure brotherly love, and kindness. How I long to live in such a place! Because I want You to live and reign in me, I ask You to teach me to forgive.

Civil government provides punishments to reduce wickedness and to discourage people from hurting each other. This is necessary and good. Guide me to understand, O Christ, that Your kingdom is a spiritual one. Your forgiveness is forever because grace is forever, and by this I am saved.

Forgive me for thinking my efforts in praying, fasting, going to church every week, or self-flagellation remove my need to let go of wrongs others have done to me. Help me recognize that my efforts to earn Your favor are a rejection of Your mercy, for mercy is shown only when no payment can be made.

Because You love me, I can love others. You've given me worldly goods in love and Your kingdom will come as I do the same with my neighbors. Show me the blessing found in giving. Let it be one of the ways I praise and return love to You.

Increase my trust that You saved me, that You received the punishment for all my sin, and that You set me free to know the comfort of the gospel. Thank You for faith that has led me to You. Now let my works of love declare my faith.

Send me to people who will benefit by receiving the love I have for You. Inspire me to be committed to the welfare of the world because You showed such boundless love for me. Bring me into Your kingdom as I try to live as You lived. Amen.

6. Forgive our sins, O Lord, that they
   No more may vex us, day by day,
   As we forgive their trespasses
   Who unto us have done amiss;
   Thus let us dwell in charity,
   And serve each other willingly.
   (Luther 1884q)

* * *

14. Hence the substance of this Gospel is that no mortal is so high, nor will ever ascend so high, who will not have occasion to fear that he may become the very lowest. On the other hand, no mortal lies so low or can fall so low, to whom the hope is not extended that he may become the highest; because here all human merit is abolished and God's goodness alone is praised. (Vol. 2:111)

* * *

Prayer for Matthew 20:1–16
The Laborers in the Vineyard

[Jesus said], "For the kingdom of heaven is like a landowner who went out early in the morning to hire men to work in his vineyard. He agreed to pay them a denarius for the day and sent them into his vineyard.

About the third hour he went out and saw others standing in the marketplace doing nothing. He told them, 'You also go and work in my vineyard, and I will pay you whatever is right.' So they went.

He went out again about the sixth hour and the ninth hour and did the same thing. About the eleventh hour he went out and found still others standing around. He asked them, 'Why have you been standing here all day long doing nothing?'

"'Because no one has hired us,' they answered.

"He said to them, 'You also go and work in my vineyard.'

"When evening came, the owner of the vineyard said to his foreman, 'Call the workers and pay them their wages, beginning with the last ones hired and going on to the first.'

"The workers who were hired about the eleventh hour came and each received a denarius. So when those came who were hired first, they expected to receive more. But each one of them also received a denarius. When they received it, they began to grumble against the landowner. 'These men who were hired last worked only one hour,' they said, 'and you have made them equal to us who have borne the burden of the work and the heat of the day.'

"But he answered one of them, 'Friend, I am not being unfair to you. Didn't you agree to work for a denarius? Take your pay and go. I want to give the man who was hired last the same as I gave you. Don't I have the right to do what I want with my own money? Or are you envious because I am generous?'

"So the last will be first, and the first will be last." (NIV, 1984)

Teacher of Truth,

Sometimes I try to make more out of Your parables than You intended to teach in them. In the same way, I make faith more complex than I should. Open my mind to the simplicity of Your message and lead me to praise Your infinite goodness and mercy.

Why do I keep missing the point that Your reward comes, not because of my efforts, but because of Your grace? Lead me to rest in Your compassion rather than to participate in the futile work of self-justification. Forgive me for criticizing others because I don't see them exerting the same effort I make to serve You. Teach me to serve You because You are good and merciful, not because I think I should receive a greater reward.

No matter how much I've done in Your service, may I always count myself as one of those hired in the last hour, who realize my efforts do nothing to warrant Your overwhelming generosity. I don't always recognize that I, in an outward display of my spirituality, or even of my suffering, might be expecting greater rewards than others. Save me from this kind of pride.

Then there are times when I compare myself to others and I think I'm a poor excuse for a disciple. I don't suffer much and the cross I bear doesn't seem to be as heavy as the one I think Christians are supposed to carry. I feel like I'm closer to last in holiness than to first. Help me not to measure myself against others. I want to grow in purity just for the joy of pleasing You.

How can the meager reward of one day's pay, or one life's blessings, compare with experiencing the magnitude of the Master's goodness? Forgive me for my shallow understanding and for my inadequate trust in You.

As I learn to discipline myself in prayer, study, and worship, I ask that I won't ever think these actions lift me higher than any other soul before You. I am only one small step away from falling into sin, just like everyone else. And yet, no matter how far I might fall, there is no place too low that You cannot lift me and restore me to Yourself. Amen.

8. Couldst thou earn thine own salvation,
   Useless were my death and passion;
   Wilt thou thine own helper be?
   No meet table is this for thee.

9. If thou this believest truly,
   And confession makest duly,
   Thou a welcome guest art here,
   This rich banquet thy soul shall cheer.
   (Huss 1884)

* * *

87. What does it signify that the apostles, without command, put their garments on the colt? .... Paul says in one of his epistles, we shall put on, Christ, by which he doubtless wishes to show that good works are the garments of the Christians, by which Christ is honored and glorified before all people.... By this he means to show that good works are garments in which we walk before the people, honorably and well adorned. The examples of the apostles are the best and noblest above all the saints, they instruct us best, and teach Christ most clearly; therefore they should not, like the rest, lie on the road, but on the colt, so that Christ may ride on them and the colt go under them. We should follow these examples, praise Christ with our confession and our life. (Vol. 1:53–54)

* * *

Prayer for Matthew 21:1–9
Jesus' Entry into Jerusalem

When they had come near Jerusalem and had reached Bethphage, at the Mount of Olives, Jesus sent two disciples, saying to them, "Go into the village ahead of you, and immediately you will find a donkey tied, and a colt with her; untie them and bring them to me. If anyone says anything to you, just say this, 'The Lord needs them.' And he will send them immediately." This took place to fulfill what had been spoken through the prophet, saying, "Tell the daughter of Zion, Look, your king is coming to you, humble, and mounted on a donkey, and on a colt, the foal of a donkey."

The disciples went and did as Jesus had directed them; they brought the donkey and the colt, and put their cloaks on them, and he sat on them. A very large crowd spread their cloaks on the road, and others cut branches from the trees and spread them on the road. The crowds that went ahead of him and that followed were shouting, "Hosanna to the Son of David! Blessed is the one who comes in the name of the Lord! Hosanna in the highest heaven!" (NRSV)

Triumphant and Blessed Lord,

You are the Promised One sent by God, but no one anticipated You would be like this. You, the Son who is one with the Father, were more like the beast of burden that carried a man into Jerusalem than a powerful commander riding on a stallion. You came in humble service to carry the weight of my sin. You opened the gates of the Kingdom to me. Open my heart and teach me to serve my neighbor in humility the same way You served me.

I try to make myself look better in Your sight by obeying the law and observing religious rituals, yet I don't do these thing very well. I need You to be the reigning power in my life. I cannot drive sin, death, and hell away from me by good works or spiritual deeds. I want to trust that You have laid aside all wrath for the wrongs I have done so I will no longer fear for the future of my soul. Draw me to trust in Your goodness and love and let this faith give rise to love and compassion for all people.

Sometimes I think I can do something good for God. How can I help God who needs nothing? I can only help my neighbor who is in need. Lead me to focus my life on living and dying for the good of my family, for those over me, for those under me, and for those in need of my help.

In faith, I accept that You have given Yourself to me. Through love, I will give myself to my neighbor. Grant that I may submit to Your reign in my life so that You can bring forth godly and merciful actions. Let me become a holy instrument in Your hands.

Lord, I often get power and majesty confused with Your reign. Open my eyes to see your presence in the poor and needy. Give me a spirit willing to let You guide my path. Accept this offering from my heart, my praise and thanksgiving. Amen.

5. The Father's Son, God everblest,
   In the world became a guest;
   He leads us from this vale of tears,
   And makes us in his kingdom heirs.
   Hallelujah!

6. He came to earth so mean and poor,
   Man to pity and restore,
   And make us rich in heaven above,
   Equal with angels through his love.
   Hallelujah!
   (Luther 1884a)

* * *

19. Now the wedding garment is Christ himself, which is put on by faith, as the Apostle says in Rom. 13, 14: "Put ye on the Lord Jesus Christ." Then the garment gives forth a lustre of itself, that is, faith in Christ bears fruit of itself, namely, love which works through faith in Christ. These are the good works, that also flash forth from faith, and entirely gratuitously do they go forth, they are done alone for the good of our neighbor; otherwise they are heathenish works, if they flow not out of faith; they will later come to naught and be condemned, and be cast into the outermost darkness. (Vol. 5:234)

* * *

Prayer for Matthew 22:1–14
The Parable of the Wedding Banquet

And Jesus answered and spoke to them again by parables and said: "The kingdom of heaven is like a certain king who arranged a marriage for his son, and sent out his servants to call those who were invited to the wedding; and they were not willing to come. Again, he sent out other servants, saying, 'Tell those who are invited, "See, I have prepared my dinner; my oxen and fatted cattle are killed, and all things are ready. Come to the wedding."'

But they made light of it and went their ways, one to his own farm, another to his business. And the rest seized his servants, treated them spitefully, and killed them. But when the king heard about it, he was furious. And he sent out his armies, destroyed those murderers, and burned up their city. Then he said to his servants, 'The wedding is ready, but those who were invited were not worthy. Therefore go into the highways, and as many as you find, invite to the wedding.' So those servants went out into the highways and gathered together all whom they found, both bad and good. And the wedding hall was filled with guests.

"But when the king came in to see the guests, he saw a man there who did not have on a wedding garment. So he said to him, 'Friend, how did you come in here without a wedding garment?' And he was speechless. Then the king said to the servants, 'Bind him hand and foot, take him away, and cast him into outer darkness; there will be weeping and gnashing of teeth.' For many are called, but few are chosen." (NKJV)

Love of my Life,

Why do You hide the mystery of the kingdom of heaven in Your parables? Open my mind to the spiritual meanings of Your teachings beyond what my eyes and ears can see, and show me how this one applies to me.

I too am invited to a wedding feast offered by the heavenly Father. He promises to feed and nourish my faith through meditation on Christ and the examples of faithful people like Abraham, yet I confess that I resist believing these things will bless me. I insist there are more important things to do that will bring me honor and provide all the things I want to possess. Worst of all, I reject the Father's messengers who teach me things that are different from what has been taught in the past. I am blind to the true riches, and for this I am sorry. Let the light of faith in You illuminate the way.

Let the good works that I do for my neighbor arise because I know the Father in heaven is interested in me, cares deeply for me, and knows what is best for me. Without this garment of faith in You, I will be naked and seen for who I am, someone interested only in myself. Kindle within me a faith bolstered by the graciousness of the Bridegroom and the joy of participating in the wedding feast. Let me then share my enthusiasm as I invite others to join in the feast of eternal riches, which are forgiveness of sins, comfort, strength, and renewal of the Holy Spirit through participation in the Church.

As I partake in the marriage feast, unite Your divine nature with my own so that I can appreciate the Father's good will toward His creation. I pledge not only my gifts and my works, but my whole heart in the same way You gave Yourself to me. What's mine is Yours, and what's Yours is mine, an exchange that I'm humbly aware is quite unequal: My death sentence for Your life, my sins for Your righteousness, my condemnation for Your salvation.

Like so many Christians, I want union with You without giving all that is mine to the relationship. The world has taught me to trust no one. Forgive me, Jesus. Wash me of my sin and become my righteousness. Purify me with the Word and sacraments. Clothe me with Yourself. Give me a faith that shows itself in bearing fruit, displaying the luster of loving works that benefit my neighbor. I want to give You all of me without fear, without reservation, without hesitation. My understanding is so inadequate. I want to drink in and taste the vastness of Your goodness.

Adorn me with the wedding garment of faith that always reveals itself in works of love. Teach me how to experience You and Your riches with laughter and eternal joy. May I live only in ways that are pleasing to You, my Bridegroom and my truest Love. Amen.

7. To me he spake: cling fast to me,
   Thou'lt win a triumph worthy;
   I wholly give myself for thee;
   I strive and wrestle for thee;
   For I am thine, thou mine also;
   And where I am thou art. The foe
   Shall never more divide us.
   (Luther 1884e)

* * *

8. This is written for our consolation, in order that we who believe in Christ should know that we have a wisdom that far surpasses all other wisdom; a strength and righteousness, which are not to be compared with any human strength or righteousness; for against the Holy Spirit no counsel can prevail. (Vol. 5:297–8)

* * *

Prayer for Matthew 22:15–22
The Question about Paying Taxes

Then the Pharisees went and plotted to entrap him in what he said. So they sent their disciples to him, along with the Herodians, saying, "Teacher, we know that you are sincere, and teach the way of God in accordance with truth, and show deference to no one; for you do not regard people with partiality. Tell us, then, what you think. Is it lawful to pay taxes to the emperor, or not?"

But Jesus, aware of their malice, said, "Why are you putting me to the test, you hypocrites? Show me the coin used for the tax." And they brought him a denarius. Then he said to them, "Whose head is this, and whose title?" They answered, "The emperor's." Then he said to them, "Give therefore to the emperor the things that are the emperor's, and to God the things that are God's." When they heard this, they were amazed; and they left him and went away. (NRSV)

Sovereign God and Lord,

I'm too much like the children of Israel who wanted a king who would tell them what they should and shouldn't do. Sometimes that's easier than thinking for myself. Yet the deceit of leaders, both religious and secular, is disturbing. Who can be trusted? By the wisdom of the Holy Spirit, let me use the Word and commandments as my guide. Free me from the inclination to place absolute trust in people who are in authority. Lead me to accept that true freedom will come when I have placed my trust entirely in You as You continue to reveal Yourself to my heart and mind.

The wisdom of the world is no match for divine wisdom. Like the Pharisees opposed Your Son, those who rise up against the Gospel will become caught in their own trap. Yet fighting against authority doesn't gain Christian freedom when we overlook faith and love. Empower me as I navigate this delicate balance.

Help me understand that the practice of religion is not in opposition to the affairs of the state. Each has an important role to play. Inspire governments to act in the best interests of their people. Give them wisdom to bring about peace in just ways. I pray that leaders will be elected in my nation and around the world who are dedicated to serving the needs of the people.

Open my ears to listen to the Holy Spirit. Help me discern who is trustworthy and who has placed self-interest above the common good. When I see leaders serving unjustly, temper my protests so they will be voiced in peaceful and orderly ways. If difficulties arise because I stand up for people who are treated unfairly, give me confidence that You are my strength and my fortress.

When I'm encouraged by others to react with physical force against evil, guide my thoughts to remember Jesus. Lead me to follow his example and imitate his response to evil. Give me faith that leaves all vengeance in Your hands, even if I must suffer harm at another's hand.

Make me confident that the good news will never die but instead will gain power wherever it is opposed. Many more will come to faith because of the attention drawn to the resistance. Let me be more wary of prosperity more than persecution because good days lull me into complacency and self-interest.

Be with me in my dealings with authority. Let them have what they need, but to You I will give my heart. I will place my confidence only in the Lord, and say: *O Lord, You are my life, my soul and body, my goods and possessions, and all that is mine. Direct and ordain it all according to Your divine will. In You I trust, in You I believe. You will surely not desert me in perilous undertakings with people I do not trust. If You know the interaction will be good for me, then see to it that they are true to me; if You see that it will not help me, then let me be content and may Your will be done.* Amen.
(Italics: Luther 1983, Vol. 5:302)

6. Kill thou not out of evil will,
   Nor hate, nor render ill for ill;
   Be patient and of gentle mood,
   And to thy foe do thou good.
   Have mercy, Lord.

8. Steal not; oppressive acts abhor;
   Nor wring their life-blood from the poor;
   But open wide thy loving hand
   To all the poor in the land.
   Have mercy, Lord.
   (Luther 1884t)

* * *

13. Therefore, when the law impels one against love, it ceases and should no longer be a law; but where no obstacle is in the way, the keeping of the law is a proof of love, which lies hidden in the heart. Therefore ye have need of the law, that love may be manifested; but if it cannot be kept without injury to our neighbor, God wants us to suspend and ignore the law. (Vol. 5:175)

* * *

Prayer for Matthew 22:34–46
The Greatest Commandment

But when the Pharisees heard that Jesus had silenced the Sadducees, they gathered themselves together. One of them, a lawyer, asked Him a question, testing Him, "Teacher, which is the great commandment in the Law?"

And He said to him, "'You shall love the Lord your God with all your heart, and with all your soul, and with all your mind.' This is the great and foremost commandment. The second is like it, 'You shall love your neighbor as yourself.' On these two commandments depend the whole Law and the Prophets."

Now while the Pharisees were gathered together, Jesus asked them a question: "What do you think about the Christ, whose son is He?" They said to Him, "The son of David."

He said to them, "Then how does David in the Spirit call Him 'Lord,' saying, 'The Lord said to my lord, "Sit at my right hand, until I put your enemies beneath your feet"'?

"If David then calls Him 'Lord,' how is He his son?" No one was able to answer Him a word, nor did anyone dare from that day on to ask Him another question. (NASB)

Fountain of Love in my Heart,

I know You've told me to love my neighbor. But I don't like some of my neighbors. What am I supposed to do? I'm grateful that You set up laws because I wouldn't know what is right or what is wrong in my actions without them nor would I have a measuring stick to discern if I am loving You with all my heart and my neighbor as myself. Yet these are external efforts, and I need You to help me want good for my neighbor from my heart. Please guide me to a better understanding of this law so I can follow it in spirit and not just deed.

Many of Your laws clearly bless us when we obey them. But I admit that some confuse me. When I question the value of following one of Your commands, inspire me to comply because I love and trust You above all things. At the same time, guide me in abandoning any command that opposes the love of my neighbor, since love sets aside any commandment that makes the journey unbearable for others.

I know this is a frightening thing for many to imagine, giving authority to each person to choose the laws they want to follow. Yet You have written Your law on my heart. Forgive me, Lord, when I get angry with people who don't follow the laws the way I think they should. You have more right to be angry with me when I ignore Your command to love my neighbor but instead I follow my own agenda. I want to make my love for You known through following Your commands rather than following them to prove how good I am. Change my will to mirror Your perfect will.

Precious Lord, how did You ever fulfill the law perfectly? And why would You ever take my sin upon Yourself, covering my shame with Your cloak as a free gift? I can't even follow the Ten Commandments and good works don't excuse bad behavior. So what is a person supposed to do except run to You for help, as I do right now? Help me, Jesus. Free me from the fear all these laws bring to me.

Awaken Your Holy Spirit within me. I want to become a new person. I want to do a better job of following Your instruction. Yet I cannot do this in my own power. Fill me with Your love so that I may serve You in righteous living and assure me that You will have mercy on me, a sinner.

Now that You have explained the heart of the Law, free me from its hold on my attention. Turn my focus to You and Your relationship to the Almighty God, for no jealous God would make someone His equal or share His glory with another. Let this knowledge become the motivation from which I follow You and Your commands. Amen.

11. God these commandments gave, therein
    To show thee, son of man, thy sin,
    And make thee also well perceive
    How man for God ought to live.
    Have mercy, Lord.
    (Luther 1884t)

* * *

8. Therefore the whole dispute consists in this, that the false saints quarreled with the true saints about the worship of God and good works, the former saying this is divine worship; the latter saying no, it is idolatry and unbelief. Thus it has been from the beginning, and it will also continue unto the end. (Vol. 1:227)

* * *

Prayer for Matthew 23:34–39
Woes to the Pharisees

[Jesus said] "Therefore I send you prophets, sages, and scribes, some of whom you will kill and crucify, and some you will flog in your synagogues and pursue from town to town, so that upon you may come all the righteous blood shed on earth, from the blood of righteous Abel to the blood of Zechariah son of Barachiah, whom you murdered between the sanctuary and the altar.

"Truly I tell you, all this will come upon this generation.

"Jerusalem, Jerusalem, the city that kills the prophets and stones those who are sent to it! How often have I desired to gather your children together as a hen gathers her brood under her wings, and you were not willing! See, your house is left to you, desolate. For I tell you, you will not see me again until you say, 'Blessed is the one who comes in the name of the Lord.'" (NRSV)

Protective Lord,

What is it about a prophet that stirs up great resistance in religious people? Help me to see that prophets clarify Your will no matter what's been taught for centuries. Forgive me if I am one who persecutes teachers that are listening to the Holy Spirit rather than holding to tradition. Grant courage and perseverance to those who come to reveal the true knowledge of You and Your will.

Forgive me for trusting in reason and closing my ears to the people You are sending to teach me. Yet, how am I supposed to know who is sent by You and who isn't? Give me wisdom to discern which people I should listen to, which preachers to pay attention to, and which authors to believe. Lead me to rely less on my mind and more on my heart for accepting the truth as taught by You.

Enrich my understanding so I stop clinging to outward displays of religious ceremony and ritual that create a false sense of holiness. Continue to send prophets to remind Your people that You didn't command these things. Instead, You commanded us to love our neighbors. Free me from fears that come when I consider deviating from centuries of tradition. Lead me to faith and increase my desire to care for my neighbors.

Guide Your people to recognize that we are one in You, from saints of the past to newborns today. Unite us in the way we define service and good works carried out in Your precious name. Lead us to rely on what is found in Scripture but not to add more to it. Forgive us for every evil we commit against You while You show us only love and goodness. Thank You for Your intense desire to bring us together under Your protective wing, even though we fail so miserably to trust in You.

I deserve Your angry words when I show a lack of trust. Still, You comfort me by expressing Your longing to care for me. My soul is like the chick that scurries away from the hen while Satan and evil spirits circle overhead like buzzards, waiting to attack. Give me refuge under the wing of Your righteousness, for nothing I say or do will hide me or keep me safe from judgment. I will cling to You; for the good You chose to do covers me and keeps me safe.

Grant that Your prophets today might pray and be heard: *O Lord God, we are too greatly torn to atoms, too sorely crushed; O Christ, our Lord, we poor miserable people are too desert-like and too forsaken in these last days of Your wrath. Our shepherds are like wolves, our watchmen are traitors, our protectors are enemies, our fathers are murderers, and our teachers mislead us. Oh! Oh! Oh! When, when, when will Your severe wrath have an end? Bless us in knowing we will all see and hear You again, and when we do, we will all be shouting, "Blessed is He that comes in the name of the Lord!" May God grant this time be near at hand.* Amen.
(Italics: Luther 1983, Vol. 1:237)

3. May God bestow on us His grace and blessing,
   That, his holy footsteps tracing,
   We walk as brethren dear in love and union,
   Nor repent this sweet communion.
   Kyri' eleison!*

   Let not us the Holy Ghost forsake;
   May he grant that we the right way take;
   That thy poor church may see
   Days of peace and unity.
   Kyri' eleison!
   (Luther 1884m)

   * Kyri' eleison! is a transliteration of the Greek for "Lord, have mercy."

* * *

22. Now it is high time for him to run and flee, who is able to flee; let everything he has behind and depart; the sooner the better; not with his feet but with his heart, in such a way that he will be rid of the abomination and enter the kingdom of Christ through faith. But to do this reason and a keen insight are needed rightly to discern the abomination. It cannot be seen in any way better than when we compare it to Christ who teaches, as stated above, that we are reconciled to God, and are saved through his blood. (Vol. 5:373)

* * *

Prayer for Matthew 24:15-28
The Great Tribulation

[Jesus said], "So when you see standing in the holy place 'the abomination that causes desolation,' spoken of through the prophet Daniel—let the reader understand—then let those who are in Judea flee to the mountains. Let no one on the roof of his house go down to take anything out of the house. Let no one in the field go back to get his cloak. How dreadful it will be in those days for pregnant women and nursing mothers! Pray that your flight will not take place in winter or on the Sabbath. For then there will be great distress, unequaled from the beginning of the world until now—and never to be equaled again. If those days had not been cut short, no one would survive, but for the sake of the elect those days will be shortened. At that time if anyone says to you, 'Look, here is the Christ!' or, 'There he is!' do not believe it. For false Christs and false prophets will appear and perform great signs and miracles to deceive even the elect—if that were possible. See, I have told you ahead of time.

"So if anyone tells you, 'There he is, out in the desert,' do not go out; or, 'Here he is, in the inner rooms,' do not believe it. For as lightning that comes from the east is visible even in the west, so will be the coming of the Son of Man. Wherever there is a carcass, there the vultures will gather. (NIV, 1984)

Redeemer of my Soul,

The foundations of the world shake when my religious traditions are threatened. Conflict erupts within me and among my brothers and sisters in the faith. You are the cause. The kingdom I've grown up in has been constructed out of laws, offerings, and church formalities that make me feel secure. I've been convinced I should accept what earthly rulers tell me I must do. I don't know any other way. Why must You, O Christ, bring change of seismic proportions? Teach me how You were able to let God reign in You, and, in doing so, You fulfilled the Law. Lead me to a place where You alone reign in me.

Your chosen people of Israel killed and persecuted the prophets who spoke against tradition. I see Christians doing the same to God's messengers of change today. Help me understand that loving, serving, and worshiping You is not about clinging to the forms of the past. It's about You coming into my life and how I respond to You. Bring to an end any confidence I've placed in practices and rituals that are unnecessary. I want to move forward in my trust in You and Your teachings.

Make me Your holy temple. Lead me away from thinking works of any kind replace You in removing sin, death, or misfortune, for this is the abomination of desolation the prophet Daniel foretold. I want to know the freedom that can only be found in You. Bring me under the reign of God, and bless me with Your Holy Spirit who brings the treasures and riches of God.

Rule over my conscience, Lord Jesus. Send me fleeing from those things and those people that draw me away from the foundation of faith in You. Steer me away from dependence on added requirements that lessen my trust in Your blood shed for me. Let me not be fooled into thinking You want me to leave society to enter a life of seclusion. Instead, guide me to live openly the way You and the apostles lived so that I will share the good news with others.

Lord, I have a tendency to follow what others tell me to do because they appear certain they possess You and the right formulas to meet You. Yet, just because people gather together and feast does not mean I should join them. Give me faith that as long as I am searching for You, I will find You, for this is what You have promised. Amen.

3. Thanks be to God, who from the pit
   Snatched us, when it was gaping;
   Our souls, like birds that break the net,
   To the blue skies escaping;
   The snare is broken—we are free!
   The Lord our helper praiséd be,
   The God of earth and heaven.
   (Luther 1884h)

* * *

24. For there are certainly souls who are joyfully and with a good conscience awaiting the judgment of Christ; for they are in the rank and fellowship of those who believe in Christ, and who show fruits of faith through charity and beneficence toward the poor, or through patience in suffering with them. For, as I have said, he who does not have faith will not do works of mercy to Christians, but he who does them, will do them because he believes that he has a faithful Savior and Redeemer in Christ, who has reconciled him to God. Therefore he must have also a kind, loving heart toward his neighbors, even toward his enemies, and serve them in every time of need. (Vol. 5:390)

* * *

Prayer for Matthew 25:31–46
Separating the Sheep and Goats

[Jesus said] "When the Son of Man comes in his glory, and all the angels with him, then he will sit on the throne of his glory. All the nations will be gathered before him, and he will separate people one from another as a shepherd separates the sheep from the goats, and he will put the sheep at his right hand and the goats at the left.

"Then the king will say to those at his right hand, 'Come, you that are blessed by my Father, inherit the kingdom prepared for you from the foundation of the world; for I was hungry and you gave me food, I was thirsty and you gave me something to drink, I was a stranger and you welcomed me, I was naked and you gave me clothing, I was sick and you took care of me, I was in prison and you visited me.'

Then the righteous will answer him, 'Lord, when was it that we saw you hungry and gave you food, or thirsty and gave you something to drink? And when was it that we saw you a stranger and welcomed you, or naked and gave you clothing? And when was it that we saw you sick or in prison and visited you?'

And the king will answer them, 'Truly I tell you, just as you did it to one of the least of these who are members of my family, you did it to me.'

"Then he will say to those at his left hand, 'You that are accursed, depart from me into the eternal fire prepared for the devil and his angels; for I was hungry and you gave me no food, I was thirsty and you gave me nothing to drink, I was a stranger and you did not welcome me, naked and you did not give me clothing, sick and in prison and you did not visit me.'

Then they also will answer, 'Lord, when was it that we saw you hungry or thirsty or a stranger or naked or sick or in prison, and did not take care of you?' Then he will answer them, 'Truly I tell you, just as you did not do it to one of the least of these, you did not do it to me.' And these will go away into eternal punishment, but the righteous into eternal life." (NRSV)

Hidden Lord,

Your words are as frightening as they are comforting. You spoke them in hopes that some will be helped. Awaken me to see the connection my actions play in bringing long lasting reward or wrath. It's so easy to set aside the thought that one day I'll be standing before You, trying to explain what I've done with my life as a sinner for whom You died. I know I'm supposed to feel confident in Your grace, but I can't help wondering if I have done enough. Help me recognize that believing in You and loving You triggers acts of kindness for others. Let my acts of love and kindness display my trust in You.

I understand how the good works You mention in the Scripture are the positive flow coming out of the commandment—that I should not kill or be angry with my neighbor. Forgive me if I think You've asked me to do anything different from what unbelievers do to take care of each other.

I am comforted when I think of myself as a member of Your family. Will Your judgment will be greater against persons outside the family who persecute Your own? What about brothers and sisters who fail to love each other? Too often, I fail to remember that treating my Christian brothers and sisters poorly is also unacceptable in Your sight. I plead guilty to such offenses. You are in them as You are in me. Forgive me for treating You poorly, O Christ. Lead me to see You in every person.

I have heard and received the gospel, yet accepting alone doesn't make me righteous. Keep me from thinking that because I have been blessed to receive the gospel that this makes me first in Your sight. I don't want to fool myself and end up being the last. Inspire me to give my possessions to ministers and teachers of the Word so the gospel can be spread and our nation will not be overcome by evil.

I want to be kind and merciful for Your sake because I have seen the goodness of God and because I know the mercy You have shown me. Comfort me as I hope and wait and serve, until the day You come again. Bring thoughts of peace and joy to me as I await Your return. Amen.

> Thy servants help whom thou, O God,
> Hast ransomed with that precious blood;
> Grant that we share the heav'nly rest
> With the happy saints eternally blest.
> Help us, O Lord, from age to age,
> And bless thy chosen heritage.
> Nourish and keep them by thy power,
> And lift them up for evermore.
> (Luther 1884l)

* * *

2. For here we see that many persons received the poor man, as though his distress were their own, bringing him to Jesus to be helped. By this, both faith and love are shown to us. Faith, in that they had heard of the Lord before, that he was kind and compassionate, and helped all those who came to him. For the Word must first have been heard, and must first have entered the human heart, showing us the mercy of God in such a way that we depend upon it. (Vol. 4:372)

* * *

Prayer for Mark 7:31–37
Jesus Heals a Man Deaf and Mute

Again, departing from the region of Tyre and Sidon, He came through the midst of the region of Decapolis to the Sea of Galilee. Then they brought to Him one who was deaf and had an impediment in his speech, and they begged Him to put His hand on him. And He took him aside from the multitude, and put His fingers in his ears, and He spat and touched his tongue. Then, looking up to heaven, He sighed, and said to him, "Ephphatha," that is, "Be opened."

Immediately his ears were opened, and the impediment of his tongue was loosed, and he spoke plainly. Then He commanded them that they should tell no one; but the more He commanded them, the more widely they proclaimed it. And they were astonished beyond measure, saying, "He has done all things well. He makes both the deaf to hear and the mute to speak." (NKJV)

Enduring Savior,

I've been told that You expect me to lead unbelievers to You, and that makes me uncomfortable. Yet teach me that bringing people to You is as simple as praying for Your help in their need. I know I can do this. Inspire me to greater faith in Your kindness and compassion. I want to be so convinced of Your power that I don't hesitate to bring others to You in my prayers.

Your mercy and goodness draw me to You. Reports of God's anger and wrath drive me away. How do I resolve this inconsistency? No matter what others say I should believe, guide me to place my trust in the image of kindness You revealed. Lead me to follow Your example of unselfish love for people. I fear that I can never be that selfless. My tendency is to seek some kind of personal benefit from everything I do. Remove self-serving motives from me. Transform me so that I feel good when my neighbor benefits from Your healing and presence.

All my life, I have been taught that the gospel is found in the words written in the Bible. Yet my heart drinks in the words of those who tell me how You have treated them with kindness and mercy. I yearn to hear more about Your willingness to come to my aid and to the aid of everyone in the world. Forgive me for limiting the spread of the gospel when I don't tell others about the goodness You have brought into my life.

Inspire me to live in such a way that others are attracted to You through my faith and actions. Use me to speak of Your goodness, compassion, and mercy so those whose ears are closed to formal religion can be moved by the Holy Spirit and faith can begin. No one can be rescued from the power of sin or the fear of death simply because I trust in You. People need to trust in You for themselves. Touch their tongues with Your Spirit so they too can confess Your name and speak of Your mercy and grace.

Open my ears to listen for evidence of Your kindness, and empower me to resist the desire to listen for reports of my own wisdom, honor, and glory. Instead of praising myself and the things of this world, inspire me to sing Your praises, to glorify God, and to proclaim You alone as Savior.

O Christ, some of the people You heal will say and do things that bring harm to Your kingdom. They will teach false doctrines and souls will be cut off by their instructions. Guide me to speak the Word of Your love and compassion, for this has established faith within me. Let my life conform to this teaching as I submit my will to the service of my neighbor. Amen.

4. God saw, in His eternal grace,
   My sorrow out of measure;
   He thought upon his tenderness—
   To save was his good pleasure.
   He turn'd to me a Father's heart—
   Not small the cost—to heal my smart
   He gave his best and dearest.
   (Luther 1884e)

* * *

5. But "to feed on milk" means, to taste the favor and the kind grace of God. "To taste the goodness of God" means, to experience it in one's life. For should I preach a hundred years of God, how kind, sweet and good he is, that he condescends to help man, and I have not yet myself tasted it through experience; thus all is still in vain and no one is in this way taught to trust God rightly. From this you can conclude what a rare person a true Christian is. For there are many who say they trust in God for their daily bread; but that floats only upon the tongue and hangs in the ears; it never enters the heart where it belongs. (Vol. 4:204)

* * *

Prayer for Mark 8:1–9
Jesus Feeds Four Thousand

In those days when there was again a great crowd without anything to eat, [Jesus] called his disciples and said to them, "I have compassion for the crowd, because they have been with me now for three days and have nothing to eat. If I send them away hungry to their homes, they will faint on the way—and some of them have come from a great distance." His disciples replied, "How can one feed these people with bread here in the desert?" He asked them, "How many loaves do you have?" They said, "Seven." Then he ordered the crowd to sit down on the ground; and he took the seven loaves, and after giving thanks he broke them and gave them to his disciples to distribute; and they distributed them to the crowd. They had also a few small fish; and after blessing them, he ordered that these too should be distributed. They ate and were filled; and they took up the broken pieces left over, seven baskets full. Now there were about four thousand people. And he sent them away. (NRSV)

Source of Every Need,

You lovingly and gladly provide all that I need for this body and life. I know You watch over Your people with tender compassion. And yet, I worry about how I will survive in difficult economic times. If I don't trust You to preserve my physical body for the short time I live on earth, how can I trust You to care for my soul for all eternity?

Jesus, I want a faith that does not depend on seeing how You plan to take care of my needs ahead of time. Give me trust in You. Even though people tell me of Your goodness, please let me experience You for myself. Strengthen me in the belief that You will provide for my needs of food, clothing, and shelter.

Multitudes follow You and depend on You. They have so many needs to be met. Still, the masses don't appear concerned. Instead Your closest disciples got concerned. They could not see how they were to provide solutions in settings that appeared impossible. Help me to recognize that You allow us as Your disciples to try to find answers of our own, exhausting human wisdom, waiting until reason says, "It's impossible." Then You guide us to observe, in utter amazement, how easily You resolve what appears to us as a crisis. Give us confidence in Your unseen solutions.

Forgive me, dear Savior, for the lack of esteem I show for the Word of God when I poorly support those You have called to serve in ministry. They have physical needs too. Guide more workers to enter into the harvest fields and increase their faith so they do not fear poverty, for this can only distract them from Your work.

Lead me in faith to tithe of my income to You, for ten percent is a small portion of what You have given to me. With this You can sufficiently feed, clothe, and shelter those who do the kind of work I am not willing or able to do myself.

O Christ, Your kingdom has nothing to do with this temporal world. Your kingdom is spiritual, and when I seek it first, You will not fail to meet my bodily needs. Grant, in my trials, the vision to see my dependency on You. I want to trust in Your power to bring much out of very little. I will wait patiently for You, the Word of God, to feed me.

As I am blessed in having my bodily needs met, let me thank You and show love for You by graciously and freely serving my neighbor in the same way You served those around You. Amen.

5. Give us this day our daily bread,
   Let us be duly clothed and fed,
   And keep thou from our homes afar
   Famine and pestilence and war,
   That we may live in godly peace,
   Unvexed by cares and avarice.
   (Luther 1884q)

* * *

3. The risen Christ waits not until we ask or call on him to become his brethren. Do we here speak of merit, by which we deserve anything? What did the apostles merit? Peter denied his Lord three times; the other disciples all fled from him... He should have called them deserters, yea, betrayers, reprobates, anything but brethren. Therefore this word is sent to them through the women out of pure grace and mercy, as the apostles at the time keenly experienced, and we experience also, when we are mired fast in our sins, temptations and condemnation. (Vol. 2:217)

* * *

Prayer for Mark 16:1–8
The Resurrection of Jesus

When the Sabbath was over, Mary Magdalene, and Mary the mother of James, and Salome, bought spices, so that they might come and anoint Him. Very early on the first day of the week, they came to the tomb when the sun had risen. They were saying to one another, "Who will roll away the stone for us from the entrance of the tomb?" Looking up, they saw that the stone had been rolled away, although it was extremely large. Entering the tomb, they saw a young man sitting at the right, wearing a white robe; and they were amazed. And he said to them, "Do not be amazed; you are looking for Jesus the Nazarene, who has been crucified. He has risen; He is not here; behold, here is the place where they laid Him. But go, tell His disciples and Peter, 'He is going ahead of you to Galilee; there you will see Him, just as He told you.'" They went out and fled from the tomb, for trembling and astonishment had gripped them; and they said nothing to anyone, for they were afraid. (NASB)

Risen and Victorious Lord,

I am glad to know about Your death and resurrection, Lord, but I don't understand why You did this for me. What can I say to the One who destroyed sin, death, and hell so I can rise again to live forever with my Lord and King? Anything I say is inadequate.

You always meet me where I am. You come to my home, not requiring any apology for deserting You, denying You, or betraying You. You invite me to begin a new relationship with You. How can You be so forgiving, so unchanged by my rejection and my lack of interest? You see hope for me where I cannot see it.

I can't comprehend that You call me a brother or sister after what I've done and left undone. You are the Son of God. To be Your sibling makes me a child of God and gives me an inheritance with You in the kingdom of God. Me? A child of God? An heir? You honor me instead of heaping shame on me. Such mercy is inconceivable coming from the One who sits at the right hand of God.

When I turn my attention to the things I do that are wrong, they gain power over me again. I seem to be drawn toward what I focus on. Direct my eyes to look upon You, O Christ. Teach me to center my thoughts on You, for You show that my sin has been conquered. You have cast it aside, forgotten it, and I can experience both relief and joy. Fill me with an unquenchable desire to tell all the world of Your goodness, love, and grace.

You came for me in flesh and blood. You experienced pain, temptation, sorrow, and more. You experienced all I face in this life. Draw me to Yourself when I need comfort and aid. By the Holy Spirit, teach me to trust in Your Word. I will cling to You rather than rely on my physical senses and reason. Fill me with peace as I trust You suffered for my sins and rose from the tomb to justify me before my heavenly Father.

With great love and courage, Your friends came to serve You. As they approached the impossible task of moving an ominous stone, Your power and glory was revealed to them. As I approach overwhelming tasks of service to You, give me complete confidence that You possess power greater than all obstacles.

In tranquility and joy, I want to do Your will, loving my neighbor until the day I die when I will rise to be with You in glory. Amen.

1. Jesus Christ, who came to save,
   And overcame the grave,
   Is now arisen,
   And sin hath bound in prison.
   Kyrie eleison! [Lord have mercy.]

2. Who withoutén sin was found,
   Bore our transgression's wound.
   He is our Saviour,
   And brings us to God's favor.
   Kyrie eleison! [Lord have mercy.]
   (Luther 1884j)

* * *

69. Therefore, it depends not on the person, whoever it may be, that administers baptism or that receives it; who it is that preaches the Word or hears it. They may be saints or sinners, believers or unbelievers; if only the Word is preached and taught in its purity, then the ministry is also right, no matter who the minister may be. The office of preaching being first observed, then Christ speaks to you and me who hear the Word and desire to be Christians, admonishing us with this passage: "He that believeth and is baptized shall be saved." (Vol. 3:238–9)

* * *

Prayer for Mark 16:14–20
Jesus Commissions the Disciples

Later [Jesus] appeared to the eleven themselves as they were sitting at the table; and he upbraided them for their lack of faith and stubbornness, because they had not believed those who saw him after he had risen. And he said to them, "Go into all the world and proclaim the good news to the whole creation. The one who believes and is baptized will be saved; but the one who does not believe will be condemned. And these signs will accompany those who believe: by using my name they will cast out demons; they will speak in new tongues; they will pick up snakes in their hands, and if they drink any deadly thing, it will not hurt them; they will lay their hands on the sick, and they will recover."

So then the Lord Jesus, after he had spoken to them, was taken up into heaven and sat down at the right hand of God. And they went out and proclaimed the good news everywhere, while the Lord worked with them and confirmed the message by the signs that accompanied it. (NRSV)

Holy Mediator,

I often forget that the apostles were not perfect. Why wouldn't they believe the message the women told after they saw You? I admit that when people have shared the evidence of Your presence in their lives, I have doubted it. How frustrating that must be for You. And still, You show tolerance and patience and give only a gentle reprimand for my lack of trust.

Lead me, kind Lord, to trust that You are powerfully present in the world today. Guide me never to think I am better than others because of the beliefs I hold or the works I do. Teach me to be like You when dealing with neighbors who sin, not withholding love from them if they don't listen to me.

Without the resurrection, I might imagine that sin and death had defeated You. Give me trust that in the resurrection You became my mediator to God, taking my sin and the Father's wrath upon Yourself. Thank You, Jesus, for making it clear that You reconciled the world to the Father.

I am no longer a captive of sin and death. I am now a witness to the good news that You are alive today, bringing forgiveness and redemption for the sin of the world. In Your love, sin's power and control fade away. Increase my trust in this news so I will freely proclaim God's mercy and grace to all.

Thank You for the assurance I received in baptism that comforts me with God's divine pledge. Let me bear this seal as a testimony to my faith in You. Give me confidence that I am a child of God and an inheritor of eternal life. Magnify my desire to hear Your Word continually, for it kindles and strengthens my faith.

Help me to understand that it doesn't matter who preaches the Word or administers the sacraments, whether saint or sinner, believer or unbeliever, You are the Word. And when You are taught in purity and truth, then the ministry is right regardless of the minister.

Because You ascended to heaven, You have no limitations. The physical world is transcended and You can be with me always. Please be the Lord of my life. Amen.

5. Thus Jesus his disciples sent:
   Go, teach ye every nation,
   That lost in sin they must repent,
   And flee from condemnation:
   He that believes and is baptized,
   Obtains a mighty blessing;
   A new-born man, no more he dies,
   Eternal life possessing,
   A joyful heir of heaven.
   (Luther 1884v)

* * *

19. Behold how very richly God honors those who are despised of men, and that very gladly.... Nor could the angels find princes or valiant men to whom to communicate the good news; but only unlearned laymen, the most humble people upon earth. Could they not have addressed the high priests, who it was supposed knew so much concerning God and the angels? No, God chose poor shepherds, who, though they were of low esteem in the sight of men, were in heaven regarded as worthy of such great grace and honor. (Vol. 1:142)

* * *

Prayer for Luke 2:1–14
Jesus' Birth and Announcement to the Shepherds

In those days Caesar Augustus issued a decree that a census should be taken of the entire Roman world. (This was the first census that took place while Quirinius was governor of Syria.) And everyone went to his own town to register.

So Joseph also went up from the town of Nazareth in Galilee to Judea, to Bethlehem the town of David, because he belonged to the house and line of David. He went there to register with Mary, who was pledged to be married to him and was expecting a child. While they were there, the time came for the baby to be born, and she gave birth to her firstborn, a son. She wrapped him in cloths and placed him in a manger, because there was no room for them in the inn.

And there were shepherds living out in the fields nearby, keeping watch over their flocks at night. An angel of the Lord appeared to them, and the glory of the Lord shone around them, and they were terrified. But the angel said to them, "Do not be afraid. I bring you good news of great joy that will be for all the people. Today in the town of David a Savior has been born to you; he is Christ the Lord. This will be a sign to you: You will find a baby wrapped in cloths and lying in a manger."

Suddenly a great company of the heavenly host appeared with the angel, praising God and saying,

"Glory to God in the highest,
and on earth peace to men on whom his favor rests." (NIV, 1984)

Exalted Lord,

You are the Creator of all things. Yet You placed Yourself in a physical body, becoming subject to the flesh and human authorities. If this represents Wisdom above all things, it's beyond my comprehension. In the same way, hearing You did this for my benefit is inconceivable. Grant me insight to recognize that Your example of humility offers the clearest vision of what You want me to do in my efforts to serve You.

People who are born poor or into insignificant families go unheeded by those who eat and sleep in comfort. In the same way, You went unnoticed by those who enjoyed the security of rooms in the inn. Little has changed. The comforts of life often blind me to Your presence. Forgive and heal my inability to see You in the poor. If You wanted to honor the rich, You would have been born among them.

O Christ, I accept that You were born for me and You suffered in my place. Yet I want to believe more than that. You are more than a remarkable person in history. I want to understand the concept that You are a personal and precious gift from God, born to live within me today. Come into my humble dwelling, Prince of Peace. Let no material comfort stand in the way of welcoming You.

You sent shepherds to preach the gospel. We continue to argue today who should and who shouldn't be permitted to preach the good news. Reveal the pointlessness of thinking that any human being is responsible for faith, for only the Word can bring forth the fruit of faith. Good news is good news no matter who speaks it. Send Your Word in power so that all who hear it and receive it will be unified. Send me, like You sent the angels and shepherds, to the lowly, the despised, the unnoticed in society, for they are the ones most hungry to hear about the goodness of God. And awaken those whose money or religious practice lull them into thinking they no longer need a savior.

Through Your birth and sacrifice, You removed the burden of the Law and replaced it with one command, love. You do not need my good works, my neighbor needs them. Guide me to live my life for the purpose of doing good things for others, for this is the way You lived and died for me. Instill in me the mindfulness that every time I help a person in need, I am helping and loving You.

Having wrapped Yourself in the swaddling clothes of Scripture and laid in the manger of the Church, may I continually seek You in these places for the nourishment of my soul. Amen.

1. To shepherds, as they watched by night,
   Appeared a troop of angels bright;
   Behold the tender babe, they said,
   In yonder lowly manger laid.

2. At Bethlehem, in David's town,
   As Micah did of old make known;—
   'Tis Jesus Christ, your Lord and King,
   Who doth to all salvation bring.
   (Luther 1884v)

* * *

25. To find Christ in such poverty, and what his swaddling clothes and manger signify, are explained ... that his poverty teaches how we should find him in our neighbors, the lowliest and the most needy; and his swaddling clothes are the holy Scriptures; that in actual life we should incline to the needy; and in our studies and contemplative life only to the Scriptures; in order that Christ alone may become the man of both lives and that he may everywhere stand before us. (Vol. 1:169)

* * *

Prayer for Luke 2:15–20
The Shepherds Visit Jesus

When the angels had left them and gone into heaven, the shepherds said to one another, "Let us go now to Bethlehem and see this thing that has taken place, which the Lord has made known to us." So they went with haste and found Mary and Joseph, and the child lying in the manger. When they saw this, they made known what had been told them about this child; and all who heard it were amazed at what the shepherds told them. But Mary treasured all these words and pondered them in her heart. The shepherds returned, glorifying and praising God for all they had heard and seen, as it had been told them." (NRSV)

Loving and Empowering Word,

I want to know how I can be certain that You are established and working in my heart. Help me to recognize nine fruits that come from the Word of God and reveal Your presence within me.

The Word alone is able to produce the fruit called faith. Guide me to understand that faith doesn't arise because of the person who preaches it. Heavenly hosts may have proclaimed the good news to shepherds, but don't let that cause me to listen more readily to messengers who by appearances are holy, who are animated and entertaining rather than to those who appear less than perfect or are not as dynamic. Forgive me for assigning greater importance to the messenger than to the message. Teach me to hear the good news from anyone who shares it. Let me listen as if You Yourself are speaking the Word into my heart.

A second fruit the Word produces is unity in spirit. I confess that I often think my ideas, plans, or ways of doing things are superior to my brothers and sisters in Christ. However, I don't know all things.

Unite Your people into one mind and one will as we share Your love in the world.

Third, the power of Your Word builds a foundation of humility in all who receive You. Being human is reason enough to admit I am subject to error. Help me to resist thoughts that make me think I am better than any other person or that my shortcomings are less offensive to You.

The Word has taken root within me when the power of Your love moves me to place the needs of my neighbor above my own needs. Create in me a compassionate heart for serving others. Where You are present, the fruit of joy abounds. Let the good news inspire me to sing and dance as I live and serve those I see who are in need.

An important evidence of the Christian life is to confess and publicly witness to the Word, which is the Child in the manger. You were sent for the sake of the world. May I speak boldly of You, readily and without fear.

Assure me that I don't have to quit my day job to serve You. I am free to live to Your glory right where I am. Help me bloom where I am planted. Give me faith that offers praise and thanksgiving for the kindness and grace You have shown to me. Let me find true contentment and treasure in glorifying Your holy name.

Born in a stable, laid in a feeding trough, Your life of poverty on earth tells me I will find You in the lowliest and most needy of people. When led into uncomfortable places where I do not expect to find You, let love overcome fear so that I might recognize You and serve You.

Word of God made flesh, I pray that the image of the institutional church will be mended. Inspire believers who gather in Your name to display Your influence through their kindness. Lead me to understand how participating with other believers is truly beneficial for me. Teach me to love and honor the Church as the body of Christ. Amen.

1. From heaven above to earth I come,
   To bear good news to every home;
   Glad tidings of great joy I bring,
   Whereof I now will say and sing.
2. To you, this night, is born a child

   Of Mary, chosen Mother mild;
   This tender child of lowly birth,
   Shall be the joy of all your earth.
   (Luther 1884f)

* * *

13. For the present the prophecy of Moses may suffice which we find in Deut. 18:15 and which is quoted by the apostles ... as follows: "Jehovah thy God will raise up unto thee a prophet from the midst of thee, of thy brethren like unto me; unto him ye shall hearken." Here Moses declares that the people will no longer hearken to him, and that his teaching will end when this prophet Christ appears to whom they should hearken thenceforth. This also demonstrates that Christ was to be a light and Saviour after Moses, and no doubt better than Moses; for otherwise Moses would not have declared that his teaching and guiding would terminate, but that it would continue along with that of Christ. (Vol. 1:261–262)

* * *

Prayer for Luke 2:33–40
Jesus is Brought to the Temple

And Joseph and His mother marveled at those things which were spoken of Him. Then Simeon blessed them, and said to Mary His mother, "Behold, this Child is destined for the fall and rising of many in Israel, and for a sign which will be spoken against (yes, a sword will pierce through your own soul also), that the thoughts of many hearts may be revealed."

Now there was one, Anna, a prophetess, the daughter of Phanuel, of the tribe of Asher. She was of a great age, and had lived with a husband seven years from her virginity; and this woman was a widow of about eighty-four years, who did not depart from the temple, but served God with fastings and prayers night and day. And coming in that instant she gave thanks to the Lord, and spoke of Him to all those who looked for redemption in Jerusalem.

So when they had performed all things according to the law of the Lord, they returned to Galilee, to their own city, Nazareth. And the Child grew and became strong in spirit, filled with wisdom; and the grace of God was upon Him. (NKJV)

Promised One of God,

Like Simeon, let me recognize You will always stir some people to oppose the truth. Too often, I think my efforts should count for something toward receiving the crown of life. How little I understand about my sin. How little I understand about Your love. Help me cling to Your grace and mercy rather than trusting in the role of my works.

Your parents faithfully followed rituals prescribed in the Holy Writings. Yet, it's confusing when religious leaders today insist I must perform specific works and rituals not found in Scriptures. I'm not always certain what is important to You and what is unnecessary. Clear the religious baggage from my heart and make it a room for You to inhabit.

Like Anna, fill me with joy in knowing You are the gospel. I am humbled that You have chosen me to hear and comprehend You as God's merciful gift to the world. You are the one Moses prophesied would replace him with a new kind of teaching that all should follow. Help me understand how, if I'm following Your instruction, this makes it okay to disregard some of Moses' teachings. Teach me Your ways, O Christ. May Your example become the desire of my heart. If I suffer criticism for promoting the truth about You, let me count it a blessing.

The world will always be offended by Christ crucified and the truth. Reassure me when I am insulted because I diminish the importance of religious practices or the Ten Commandments, for Christ is not found in those places. Comfort me and encourage me when I see others oppose the good news I proclaim about You, for their resistance will confirm that I'm on the right path.

I find it a struggle to serve You when I'm committed to other callings and stations in life: as parent, child, spouse, or in my occupation. Help me to understand I am serving You when I honor and fulfill my responsibilities to those who depend upon me. I want to use the life You have given me wisely. Teach me to be a better steward of my time and possessions.

As much as I want to follow Your good and perfect will, I keep doing things I tell myself I don't want to do. I don't understand why I do this. I need Your help. I continue trying to meet the demands of the Law. I fail consistently and miserably. That's why the message of Your unconditional love is like sweet bread to a starving soul. Bless me with complete confidence in You so that sin and death lose their control over me. Come into me and supply Your power to overcome sin in my life.

You are my treasure. The more I trust in You, the less I am able to keep You to myself. Open my heart so my gratitude can overflow. Let me testify in words and in deeds so others may receive Your light. Blessed be Your holy name. Amen.

2. The Lord looked down from his high tower
   On all mankind below him,
   To see if any owned his power,
   And truly sought to know him;
   Who all their understanding bent
   To search his holy word, intent
   To do his will in earnest.

3. But none there was who walked with God,
   For all aside had slidden,
   Delusive paths of folly trod,
   And followed lusts forbidden;
   Not one there was who practiced good,
   And yet they deemed, in haughty mood,
   Their deeds must surely please him.
   (Luther 1884v)

* * *

12. The parents of Jesus lost him, going a day's journey and seeking for him among their kinsfolk and acquaintance, but found him not. They return to Jerusalem and after a search of three days he is found by them in the temple. Here God has pointed out how we can find consolation and strength in all our sorrows, and especially in these great trials, and how we can find Christ the Lord, namely by seeking him in the temple. Jesus said to his parents: "Knew ye not that I must be in my Father's house?" (Vol. 2:17–53)

* * *

Prayer for Luke 2:41–52
Twelve Year Old Jesus in the Temple

Now every year Jesus' parents went to Jerusalem for the festival of the Passover. And when he was twelve years old, they went up as usual for the festival. When the festival was ended and they started to return, the boy Jesus stayed behind in Jerusalem, but his parents did not know it. Assuming that he was in the group of travelers, they went a day's journey. Then they started to look for him among their relatives and friends. When they did not find him, they returned to Jerusalem to search for him. After three days they found him in the temple, sitting among the teachers, listening to them and asking them questions. And all who heard him were amazed at his understanding and his answers. When his parents saw him they were astonished; and his mother said to him, "Child, why have you treated us like this? Look, your father and I have been searching for you in great anxiety." He said to them, "Why were you searching for me? Did you not know that I must be in my Father's house?" But they did not understand what he said to them. Then he went down with them and came to Nazareth, and was obedient to them. His mother treasured all these things in her heart. And Jesus increased in wisdom and in years, and in divine and human favor. (NRSV)

Purifying Word,

I know I should expect trials when I bear the cross as Your disciple. Even Your mother was not exempt from despair and sorrow. Show me how fearful situations contain opportunities to trust in You. If I find myself in anxious circumstances, remind me that I don't have to endure in my own strength. When I think I have lost You, O Christ, and it seems as if grace is withdrawn from me, comfort me and keep me from despairing.

Ordinary people in Scriptures waited patiently until You came and supported them in difficult times. Help me to recognize that You guide and shape the faithful through many kinds of life experiences. Even those who demonstrate strong faith rediscover their dependence on Divine help when tragedy or failure strikes. When I am weak, be my strength, O God.

Some individuals, like Mary, have been highly revered for their faith. Too often I forget they too were people with personal weaknesses and imperfections. Rather than seeking to achieve recognition by mimicking their activities, lead me to imitate only their dependence on You.

Your parents could not find the comfort they sought when they looked in the external things of the world. The eyes of the faithful were opened to Christ in the house of God. When I feel You are absent from me, give me wisdom to search where You are always found, in a house of God, among the people of God, where the Word is heard. Let Your healing Word comfort my soul in ways the world cannot console me.

Sometimes the wisdom of children is greater than learned scholars. Guide me to accept human teachings when they are in harmony with the Word. Since it has been shown that conventions, councils, and churches are capable of making mistakes, keep me from blindly trusting the opinions and ordinances of human righteousness. Your Word is all I need.

O Christ, lead me to recognize that when I find You in Scripture, there is no wrath or displeasure, but only pure grace and sincere love for the world. In Your perfect love, cast out any fear I could have for You. Let Your presence become the desire of my heart. Amen.

6. The Son delighted to obey,
   And born of Virgin mother,
   Awhile on this low earth did stay
   That he might be my brother.
   His mighty power he hidden bore,
   A servant's form like mine he wore,
   To bind the devil captive.
   (Luther 1884e)

* * *

21. When Christ wished to bestow his gift upon Peter and others, he did not cause the fish to leap into the boat without labor or nets, as he very well might have done. But he commanded them to put out into the deep and let down their nets. That is, they should engage in the handicraft they understood and had learnt and were accustomed to, and should act as fishermen.... Thus he teaches a twofold lesson, that he will not give us anything unless we work for it, and that the things we obtain do not come from our work, but only from God's help and blessing. You are to work, but you are not to depend upon that work as if that which resulted therefrom were of your own accomplishment. (Vol. 4:151)

* * *

Prayer for Luke 5:1–11
Jesus Calls the First Disciples

Now it happened that while the crowd was pressing around Him and listening to the word of God, He was standing by the lake of Gennesaret; and He saw two boats lying at the edge of the lake; but the fishermen had gotten out of them and were washing their nets. And He got into one of the boats, which was Simon's, and asked him to put out a little way from the land. And He sat down and began teaching the people from the boat. When He had finished speaking, He said to Simon, "Put out into the deep water and let down your nets for a catch." Simon answered and said, "Master, we worked hard all night and caught nothing, but I will do as You say and let down the nets." When they had done this, they enclosed a great quantity of fish, and their nets began to break; so they signaled to their partners in the other boat for them to come and help them. And they came and filled both of the boats, so that they began to sink. But when Simon Peter saw that, he fell down at Jesus' feet, saying, "Go away from me Lord, for I am a sinful man!" For amazement had seized him and all his companions because of the catch of fish which they had taken; and so also were James and John, sons of Zebedee, who were partners with Simon. And Jesus said to Simon, "Do not fear, from now on you will be catching men." When they had brought their boats to land, they left everything and followed Him. (NASB)

Wellspring of Bountiful Fruits,

I have worked very hard in both my religious life and my secular life, only to be frustrated with the lack of results from my efforts. Help me, Lord, to be aware that when I obey Your voice, crediting all successes to you, blessings far beyond my expectations are in store. I want to trust that You provide all I receive; this knowledge is the source of contentment and rest. Those who don't trust You, but trust their own efforts, are never satisfied with what they produce, no matter how hard they work.

Teach me to focus on doing my work well rather than on the benefits I'm trying to generate for myself. Give me wisdom to rely on Your Word that speaks to my heart. When my first efforts fail to produce desirable results, encourage me that I may try again and begin trusting You for the outcome.

When results beyond what I imagine occur, may I grasp the disparity between Your awesome supremacy and myself. Do not allow the vastness of that chasm to drive me away in fear, but draw me to the enormity of Your goodness. Overcome my sense of unworthiness with the sweet consolation of grace.

As I learn how You provide physical things for me, let me also realize the paramount role You play when I participate in Your ministry. Open the way and show me how I can help grow Your kingdom. Guide me to use my talents and abilities in the work and leave the outcome to You.

One benefit of the Law is that it helps people recognize their sin. Yet as I work to grow Your kingdom, show me that declaring the Law to those who are in darkness may not be the best approach to filling the nets. This kind of preaching will get no results. Inspire me to share the consolation of the gospel, that forgiveness of sin and comfort is found in You. Gather all people into Your kingdom, Lord. And where I can help, use me. Amen.

1. May God unto us gracious be,
    And grant to us his blessing;
    Lord, show thy face to us, through thee
    Eternal life possessing:
    That all thy work and will, O God,
    To us may be revealed,
    And Christ's salvation spread abroad
    To heathen lands unsealed,
    And unto God convert them.
    (Luther 1884n)

* * *

28. Therefore, is thy brother a sinner, then cover his sin and pray for him. Dost thou publish his sins, then truly thou art not a child of your merciful Father; for otherwise thou wouldst be also as he, merciful. It is certainly true that we cannot show as great mercy to our neighbor, as God has to us; but it is the true work of the devil that we do the very opposite of mercy, which is a sure sign that there is not a grain of mercy in us. (Vol. 4:107)

* * *

Prayer for Luke 6:36–42
Teaching on Forgiveness and Judgment

[Jesus said] "Be merciful, just as your Father is merciful.

"Do not judge, and you will not be judged; do not condemn, and you will not be condemned. Forgive, and you will be forgiven; give, and it will be given to you. A good measure, pressed down, shaken together, running over, will be put into your lap; for the measure you give will be the measure you get back." He also told them a parable: "Can a blind person guide a blind person? Will not both fall into a pit? A disciple is not above the teacher, but everyone who is fully qualified will be like the teacher. Why do you see the speck in your neighbor's eye, but do not notice the log in your own eye? Or how can you say to your neighbor, 'Friend, let me take out the speck in your eye,' when you yourself do not see the log in your own eye? You hypocrite, first take the log out of your own eye, and then you will see clearly to take the speck out of your neighbor's eye." (NRSV)

Merciful Savior,

I need help understanding mercy. I especially need help giving it. Keep me from thinking I deserve forgiveness because I try to follow the rules better than others. Thank You that there is no greater model for mercy than our heavenly Father. No matter how badly I am treated, guide me to follow Your example in showing loving-kindness to my neighbor, my enemy, and to fellow Christians when they don't deserve it.

It's so difficult to forgive someone who has hurt or offended me. Yet I am grateful when others are willing to forgive when my actions have been unloving. May I never forget that I am a child of grace and You will not withdraw Your promise from me, even if I am not strong enough to forgive another. You have never required anyone to earn Your forgiveness. Still I want to learn how to let go of harm others have done to me. Help me to conduct myself in a manner that represents You and the heavenly Father. And when I succeed in extending mercy through forgiveness, let it inspire others to offer forgiveness to me in a similar way.

Judgment, condemnation, and pointing to the sins of others only prove who it is that guides these actions. I want to be a child of a merciful Father, O Christ. Remove any sense of privilege I feel when I think I have done something to justify my sitting in judgment of others. Establish within me a non-condemning attitude that encourages others in the world to become better people. Let love be the driving force in me from which good works arise and let these actions be the confirmation of a faith that is real.

Government and faith-based institutions create positions for punishing wrong actions. Stir leaders to use their authority justly, to guide and instruct their constituents by using fair measures of discipline. Punishment is truly merciful when it helps others to refrain from hurting innocent people. At the same time, negative consequences are a teaching instrument to the offender. Direct parents, teachers, and those in authority to display mercy by being willing to discipline wrong actions.

Steer me away from leaders and teachers who judge and condemn. Their students can become no better than they are. Give me wisdom to follow You, the Teacher who knows all things. Guide me to work diligently on my own faults, so I might see clearly the best way to assist others. I want to please You in showing kindness and mercy to friends, foes, and fellow Christians. Amen.

5. What though our sins are manifold?
   Supreme his mercy reigneth;
   No limit can his hand withhold,
   Where evil most obtaineth.
   He the good Shepherd is alone,
   Who Israel will redeem and own,
   Forgiving all transgression.
   (Luther 1884r)

* * *

3. Now all this has been written to the end that just as here this deed of mercy befell this widow freely and entirely of grace, only because it solicited Christ's sympathy, so from this we can draw the general rule that applies to all the merciful deeds of God, that they all overtake us without our merits, even before we seek them. He lays the foundation and makes the beginning. But why does he pity us? In this way it continues to be the grace of God. Otherwise, if we deserved it, it would not be grace. And if it be of grace, then we can say to him: Thou art a gracious God, thou also doest good to them who deserve it not. (Vol. 5:128–9)

* * *

Prayer for Luke 7:11–17
Jesus Raises the Widow's Son at Nain

Soon afterward, Jesus went to a town called Nain, and his disciples and a large crowd went along with him. As he approached the town gate, a dead person was being carried out—the only son of his mother, and she was a widow. And a large crowd from the town was with her. When the Lord saw her, his heart went out to her and he said, "Don't cry."

Then he went up and touched the coffin, and those carrying it stood still. He said, "Young man, I say to you, get up!" The dead man sat up and began to talk, and Jesus gave him back to his mother.

They were all filled with awe and praised God. "A great prophet has appeared among us," they said. "God has come to help his people." This news about Jesus spread throughout Judea and the surrounding country. (NIV,1984)

Lord of Life,

You come to us in our time of need. You even come to those who don't know You or ask for Your help. What amazing grace and compassion You show when we don't deserve Your kindnesses! Can I ever count the blessings in my life? My blessings are so numerous that I take most of them for granted. I am ashamed to think of how many things I've never thanked You for. Forgive me. Thank You.

When misfortune happens in my life or in the lives of others, use it to draw my attention to a blessing I've overlooked. Teach me to appreciate my loved ones, my health, my eyes, before they are gone. Let me thank You for things as common as the sun rising, for if it failed to rise all of life would change. Open my awareness to see the goodness of God in all things, the rain, the grain, the abundant creatures of the land.

You have the power to bring life where there is no life. I want to believe that nothing is impossible to You. When all appears lost, miracles happen. You are able to quench death like an ocean quenches a spark of fire falling into it.

Help me, Lord, to understand the spiritual meanings within the stories of the Bible. Expand my mind to consider that the soul might be seen as dead when one does not trust in You even though the body is alive. Every day, You meet death head on and overcome it to bring joy and new life.

Guide me to see how the Law is able only to condemn the dead to hell. My weak attempts to make amends for sin by following the Law simply increase the struggle. Open my ears to hear the gospel of the goodness of God, for it alone can lead me in the way of salvation. Reach out with Your healing hand to stop me from proceeding further into death, and speak Your Word into my heart so that I can be revived to new life today. Bring peace as I begin to trust You have destroyed death and removed God's wrath for any sin I have committed.

When I hear You call me to "arise," let me confess my confidence in You. Stir me to tell others of the blessings and faith You have shown to me. May I ever praise and exalt Your name. Amen.

2. Whilst in midst of death we be,
   Hell's grim jaws o'ertake us;
   Who from such distress will free.
   Who secure will make us?
   Thou only, Lord, canst do it!
   It moves thy tender heart to see
   Our great sin and misery.
   Holy and gracious God!
   Holy and mighty God!
   Holy and all-merciful Saviour!
   Thou eternal God! Let not hell dismay us
   With its deep and burning flood.
   Kyrie eleison. [Lord have mercy.]
   (Luther 1884u)

* * *

8. He says: "In honest and good hearts." Like a field, that is without a thorn or brush, cleared and spacious, as a beautiful clean place: so a heart is also cleared and clean, broad and spacious, that is without cares and avarice ... so that the Word of God truly finds lodgment there. But the field is good, not only when it lies there cleared and level, but when it is also rich and fruitful, possesses soil and is productive, and not like a stony and gravelly field. Just so is the heart that has good soil and with a full spirit is strong, fertile and good to keep the Word and bring forth fruit with patience. (Vol. 2:117-118)

* * *

Prayer for Luke 8:4–15
The Parable of the Sower

When a great crowd gathered and people from town after town came to him, [Jesus] said in a parable: "A sower went out to sow his seed; and as he sowed, some fell on the path and was trampled on, and the birds of the air ate it up. Some fell on the rock; and as it grew up, it withered for lack of moisture. Some fell among thorns, and the thorns grew with it and choked it. Some fell into good soil, and when it grew, it produced a hundredfold." As he said this, he called out, "Let anyone with ears to hear listen!" Then his disciples asked him what this parable meant. He said, "To you it has been given to know the secrets of the kingdom of God; but to others I speak in parables, so that 'looking they may not perceive, and listening they may not understand.' Now the parable is this: The seed is the word of God. The ones on the path are those who have heard; then the devil comes and takes away the word from their hearts, so that they may not believe and be saved. The ones on the rock are those who, when they hear the word, receive it with joy. But these have no root; they believe only for a while and in a time of testing fall away. As for what fell among the thorns, these are the ones who hear; but as they go on their way, they are choked by the cares and riches and pleasures of life, and their fruit does not mature. But as for that in the good soil, these are the ones who, when they hear the word, hold it fast in an honest and good heart, and bear fruit with patient endurance."
(NRSV)

Sower of the Word,

When You tell parables, I tend to think they are about other people and I fail to see myself in them. Correct my thinking. Help me understand that You are often speaking about me. In this story, You described four kinds of Christians. Am I the first kind who hears the Word but does not allow it to penetrate me because I place little or no value in it? Let me not be deceived into thinking I follow You if I let human doctrines deter me from bearing fruit. Guide me to Your example and the outcomes You desire.

Am I the second kind of Christian who receives the Word with joy, completely understanding that I am saved by Your grace and free of the Law, but then I fall away whenever I am tested by the difficulties of life? Forgive me if I am a fair-weather Christian. I want to trust and serve You no matter what is going on in my life.

Lord, I don't want to be the third kind of Christian who hears and understands the Word correctly, but the pleasures of life and the absence of persecution lull me into selfish and unfruitful living. When I am blessed with comforts, give me wisdom to see that You have given me the greatest opportunity to take part in an abundant life: giving my possessions to rescue the poor and hungry. Forgive my sin of neglect.

O Christ, there is so much more to being a Christian than hearing the Word and agreeing with it. Form me into the fourth kind of Christian who lives to show love and care to my neighbors no matter if I face trials in my life. Inspire me to live in gratitude when my living conditions are comfortable as well as when things get difficult.

Clear my heart of ill will like a farmer clears his field of debris. Plant and nurture the Word within me. I pray that the Holy Spirit will cultivate the seed of trust within me. Let me grow in confidence that You have delivered me from sin, death, and Satan. May I bring forth praise and thanksgiving and blossom with fruitful living that reveals Your goodness and glorifies Your holy name. Amen.

1. Come, Holy Spirit, Lord our God,
    And pour thy gifts of grace abroad;
    Thy faithful people fill with blessing,
    Love's fire their hearts possessing.
    O Lord, thou by thy heavenly light
    Dost gather and in faith unite
    Through all the world a holy nation
    To sing to thee with exultation,
    Hallelujah! Hallelujah!
    (Luther 1884d)

* * *

32. But Christ, the true Samaritan, takes the poor man to himself as his own, goes to him and does not require the helpless one to come to him; for here is no merit but pure grace and mercy; and he binds up his wounds, cares for him and pours in oil and wine, this is the whole Gospel from beginning to end. He pours in oil when grace is preached, as when one says: Behold thou poor man, here is your unbelief, here is your condemnation, here you are wounded and sore. Wait! All this I will cure with the Gospel. Behold, here cling firmly to this Samaritan, to Christ the Savior, he will help you, and nothing else in heaven or on earth will. You know very well that oil softens, thus also the sweet, loving preaching of the Gospel gives me a soft, mild heart toward God and my neighbor so that I risk my bodily life for the sake of Christ my Lord and his Gospel, if God and necessity require it. (Vol. 5:30)

* * *

Prayer for Luke 10:23–37
The Parable of the Good Samaritan

Then [Jesus] turned to His disciples and said privately, "Blessed are the eyes which see the things you see; for I tell you that many prophets and kings have desired to see what you see, and have not seen it, and to hear what you hear, and have not heard it."

And behold, a certain lawyer stood up and tested Him, saying, "Teacher, what shall I do to inherit eternal life?"

He said to him, "What is written in the law? What is your reading of it?"

So he answered and said, "'You shall love the Lord your God with all your heart, with all your soul, with all your strength, and with all your mind,' and 'your neighbor as yourself.'"

And He said to him, "You have answered rightly; do this and you will live."

But he, wanting to justify himself, said to Jesus, "And who is my neighbor?"

Then Jesus answered and said: "A certain man went down from Jerusalem to Jericho, and fell among thieves, who stripped him of his clothing, wounded him, and departed, leaving him half dead. Now by chance a certain priest came down that road. And when he saw him, he passed by on the other side. Likewise a Levite, when he arrived at the place, came and looked, and passed by on the other side. But a certain Samaritan, as he journeyed, came where he was. And when he saw him, he had compassion. So he went to him and bandaged his wounds, pouring on oil and wine; and he set him on his own animal, brought him to an inn, and took care of him. On the next day, when he departed, he took out two denarii, gave them to the innkeeper, and said to him, 'Take care of him; and whatever more you spend, when I come again, I will repay you.' So which of these three do you think was neighbor to him who fell among the thieves?"

And he said, "He who showed mercy on him."

Then Jesus said to him, "Go and do likewise." (NKJV)

Good and Merciful Rescuer,

Jesus, I am grateful that You have opened my eyes to see that You are the revelation of Your Father. Thank You for opening my ears to hear the gospel of the Father's goodness and receive it. I want to drink in the precious treasure of this grace You have given to me.

You teach me to judge myself by the law of love. Lead me to love You with a love high above my love for any created thing, knowing that to love You means I love to do Your will.

When I look at the Samaritan, a person despised and rejected by religious purists, let me see You, for You are the One who was despised and still helped the fallen. There are times when I too feel beaten, robbed of true life, and left for dead in sin. I don't see any effective way to help myself. Who could imagine You would come down from heaven in a human form to help me and all humanity?

I have made an effort to sanctify myself through religious rituals and traditions, but the prescriptions from Moses and preachers of the Law provide no remedy or healing for my pain. Soothe my wounds with the words of comfort I hear in the gospel. May the sight of the cross be like wine that cleanses and lifts my soul.

• You carry me like a shepherd carries his sheep. You brought me to the church to be nursed back to health. Strengthen and empower me as a member of Your church to become a comforter to others You carry in who are unable to help themselves.

I want to be a good neighbor, dear Lord. How can I do that when I am often the one who needs to be picked up and comforted? Letting You or anyone else help me when I am weak shows the two sides to being a neighbor. Help me to see we are all neighbors to each other, giver and receiver alike.

Everything You did, beloved Savior, centered around others and never around Yourself. May I turn my attention in the same direction

You did—outward—toward the needs of others. May this help me do a better job of fulfilling the law of love and bring me true life. Amen.

1. Our Father, thou in heaven above,
    Who biddest us to dwell in love,
    As brethren of one family,
    And cry for all we need to thee;
    Teach us to mean the words we say,
    And from the inmost heart to pray.
    (Luther 1884q)

* * *

10. By this he testifies also that no one but God can overcome the devil, so that again no man can boast of being able of himself to drive out either sin or the devil. Notice how he pictures the devil! He calls him a mighty giant who guards his court and home, that is, the devil not only possesses the world as his own domain, but he has garrisoned and fortified it, so that no one can take it from him.... Just as little as a house or court may withstand or contend against the tyrant who is its master, can man's free will and natural powers oppose sin and Satan, that is, not at all; but they are subject to them. And as that house must be conquered by a stronger man and thus wrested from the tyrant, so must man also be ransomed through Christ and wrested from Satan. We see again, therefore, that our works and righteousness contribute absolutely nothing toward our salvation; it is effected alone by the grace of God. (Vol. 2:160–161)

* * *

Prayer for Luke 11:14–23
Jesus and Beelzebul

Now [Jesus] was casting out a demon that was mute; when the demon had gone out, the one who had been mute spoke, and the crowds were amazed. But some of them said, "He casts out demons by Beelzebul, the ruler of the demons." Others, to test him, kept demanding from him a sign from heaven. But he knew what they were thinking and said to them, "Every kingdom divided against itself becomes a desert, and house falls on house. If Satan also is divided against himself, how will his kingdom stand? —for you say that I cast out the demons by Beelzebul. Now if I cast out the demons by Beelzebul, by whom do your exorcists cast them out? Therefore they will be your judges. But if it is by the finger of God that I cast out the demons, then the kingdom of God has come to you. When a strong man, fully armed, guards his castle, his property is safe. But when one stronger than he attacks him and overpowers him, he takes away his armor in which he trusted and divides his plunder. Whoever is not with me is against me, and whoever does not gather with me scatters. (NRSV)

Purifier of my Soul,

In my life, I have experienced Your healing power. Yet I'm like a mute person if I don't open my mouth to tell others of Your goodness and healing touch. Compel me to sing Your praises when I feel or witness Your compassionate touch. Those who are in turmoil need to know where they can turn in their despair.

I was born with the inclination to seek my own needs. I despise it that my house and kingdom are under the control of the strong arm of Satan. As much as I try to overcome the evil one who dominates my will, I fail when I depend on my power alone. Come to me. Console my despairing heart. Teach me to trust that You are stronger than the evil that wants to reign over me. Demanding signs as proof of Your power only makes a game of Your kindness. Let the truth of Your goodness be enough to strengthen my trust in You. Give me confidence that Your work on the cross has rescued me and I am not required to fight for my salvation by my own works.

The righteous actions of saints are noble and impressive. I am awed that others have served You in magnificent ways and this makes it tempting to use rules and rituals to convince myself I'm good. Nevertheless, guard me from worshiping people who have been revered for their efforts. Instead, lead me to focus on the inconceivable love You demonstrated in overcoming death. Defend me from the weapons of Satan that oppose Your grace: the doctrines and traditions of men that frighten the conscience and conceit that makes me think I can drive him out under my own power.

You came into my life and revealed Yourself to me. I want all people to experience the power of Your grace. Yet sometimes I think it's my job to convince people to trust in You. That's Your work. I pray Your mighty Spirit will increase to drive out all forces that stand in the way of faith.

As opportunities to fall into errors evolve with the times, keep me alert so I stand ready in my own house, a place where You now reign. Inspire me to gather with You through performing good works of love done in Your name. Amen.

1. Strong tower and refuge is our God,
   Right goodly shield and weapon;
   He helps us free in every need,
   That hath us now o'er taken.
   The old evil foe,
   Means us deadly woe;
   Deep guile and great might
   Are his dreaded arms in fight;
   On earth is not his equal.

2. With our own might we nothing can,
   Soon are we lost and fallen;
   But for us fights the righteous man,
   Whom God himself hath callen.
   Ask ye, Who is this?
   Jesus Christ it is,
   Our sole King and Lord,
   As God of Hosts adored;
   He holds the field forever.
   (Luther 1884s)

* * *

8. "Therefore we conclude that all law, divine and human, treating of outward conduct, should not bind any further than love goes. Love is to be the interpreter of law. Where there is no love, these things are meaningless, and law begins to do harm; as is also written in the Pope's book: "If a law or ordinance runs counter to love, it will soon come to an end." This is in brief spoken of divine and human laws. The reason for enacting all laws and ordinances is only to establish love, as Paul says, Rom. 13, 10: "Love therefore is the fulfillment of the law." Likewise verse 8: "Owe no man anything, save to love one another." For if I love my neighbor, I help him, protect him, hold him in honor, and do what I would have done to me. 9. Since then all law exists to promote love, law must soon cease where it is in conflict with love. Therefore, everything depends upon a good leader or ruler to direct and interpret the law in accordance with love." (Vol. 5:161)

* * *

Prayer for Luke 14:1–11
Jesus Heals on the Sabbath and Teaches Humility

It happened that when He went into the house of one of the leaders of the Pharisees on the Sabbath to eat bread, they were watching Him closely. And there in front of Him was a man suffering from dropsy. And Jesus answered and spoke to the lawyers and Pharisees, saying, "Is it lawful to heal on the Sabbath, or not?" But they kept silent. And He took hold of him and healed him, and sent him away. And He said to them, "Which one of you will have a son or an ox fall into a well, and will not immediately pull him out on a Sabbath day?" And they could make no reply to this.

And He began speaking a parable to the invited guests when He noticed how they had been picking out the places of honor at the table, saying to them, "When you are invited by someone to a wedding feast, do not take the place of honor, for someone more distinguished than you may have been invited by him, and he who invited you both will come and say to you, 'Give your place to this man,' and then in disgrace you proceed to occupy the last place. But when you are invited, go and recline at the last place, so that when the one who has invited you comes, he may say to you, 'Friend, move up higher'; then you will have honor in the sight of all who are at the table with you. For everyone who exalts himself will be humbled, and he who humbles himself will be exalted." (NASB)

Teacher of Love,

So many Bible stories show me that people come to You because they have heard about Your kindness and Your ability to help them. You never disappoint them. Inspire me to share my faith in Your power and mercy when I witness it for myself. Let me assure others that because God is for us we are safe from the ragings of death, the devil, and hell.

I know the Law is important and we cannot live without it. Yet the law requires a good interpreter for it to serve its function. Teach me to apply love when I interpret the Law because You gave it to serve and promote love. Without love, the Law becomes a weapon that can harm my neighbor. Guide me so I don't place rules ahead of the people they were meant to serve. When I face having to make a decision concerning whether I should help a neighbor who is in dire need or comply with religious expectations like worship, sacrament, or prayer, lead me to choose helping my neighbor.

Moses and David ignored religious rules when love and necessity demanded it. Guide me in following the spirit of the Law, not the letter. I want to follow Your example. You loved, even though by doing so, You broke a Sabbath law.

Help me to recognize that those who promote a superficial interpretation of God's laws teach falsely. In doing so, they place the Law above love. I want to learn Your way of applying the Law so I can live a life pleasing to You. If I have made promises that prevent me from being able to properly serve my neighbor or my family in love, then I have made them improperly. Release me from vows that do not serve You.

You have given to all Your followers the power, when it hinders the practice of love, to dispense with all commandments, whether they are God's laws or man's laws. Yet realizing I have been given such power does not elevate me above any other person. Teach me not to abuse this liberty, but let this freedom from the letter of the Law compel me even more to love and serve You.

Bring me humility of heart that does not want honor for myself, but wants only to help others. Give me wisdom to discern when love and necessity overrule the Law, whether divine or human. Amen.

10. Sweet henceforth shall be thy labor,
    Thou shalt truly love thy neighbor
    So shall he both taste and see
    What thy Savior hath done in thee.
    (Huss 1884)

* * *

6. The text tells us: "And they all with one consent began to make excuse."

7. That is what the Lord in Mat. 10:37–38 says: "He that loveth father or mother more than me is not worthy of me; and he that loveth son or daughter more than me is not worthy of me. And he that doth not take his cross and follow after me, is not worthy of me." Now observe how few there are who are thus experts in leaving all for Christ. For whoever will come to this supper, must esteem the Gospel above everything, body and riches, wife and child, friend and foe; yea, he must forsake everything that separates him from the Gospel, let it be as good, right and holy as it ever can be. (Vol. 4:35)

* * *

Prayer for Luke 14:16–24
The Parable of the Invitation to the Great Feast

Then Jesus said to him, "Someone gave a great dinner and invited many. At the time for the dinner he sent his slave to say to those who had been invited, 'Come; for everything is ready now.' But they all alike began to make excuses. The first said to him, 'I have bought a piece of land, and I must go out and see it; please accept my regrets.' Another said, 'I have bought five yoke of oxen, and I am going to try them out; please accept my regrets.' Another said, 'I have just been married, and therefore I cannot come.' So the slave returned and reported this to his master. Then the owner of the house became angry and said to his slave, 'Go out at once into the streets and lanes of the town and bring in the poor, the crippled, the blind, and the lame.' And the slave said, 'Sir, what you ordered has been done, and there is still room.' Then the master said to the slave, 'Go out into the roads and lanes, and compel people to come in, so that my house may be filled. For I tell you, none of those who were invited will taste my dinner.'" (NRSV)

Host of the Great Dinner,

So many people have been invited to feast on the rich food of the gospel, which is You, O Christ. You removed all costs to participate in this supper and we are free to enjoy the Father's treasures. You fulfilled the penalty for the sin of the world; You redeemed me and all believers. I believe in Your birth, death, and resurrection. I rejoice that I have been baptized. I am Yours. Teach me to prize You more than anything I possess.

Yes, I accept Your invitation with all my heart. Thank You for the comfort and strength You offer in the sacrament of Your body and blood, given in bread and wine, for they quench the thirst of my soul and bring eternal life.

Sometimes I mistakenly think obedience to the Law, the Church, or holding a religious position secures my eternal future. Or that working to cultivate and harvest in the fields of the Church is more than enough. Forgive me if I assume that because I'm one of Your chosen people, this excuses me from accepting an invitation to participate with others in the feast You offer today.

Too often I let others convince me that instead of following You, working and accumulating possessions is the best way to feast. Forgive me for believing human wisdom instead of You. Although You want to me to care for my family, help me to understand the deeper implications of Your call that places it above obligations to my family. Grant me faith that You are the true gospel who is more anxious to give than I am to receive.

Lord, it's just so hard to understand that if I am willing to give up my body and riches, spouse, children, or friends, that You will return them a hundredfold. But I'm not alone in my doubts. Look at all the leaders of the Church who fear giving up their power, influence, and possessions because they see no other way to support their obligations. Bless them and me with trust in the Word of the cross. Lead me to the point where I can give up a worldly outlook on what brings life. Teach me to believe that nothing will be lost that is given up for the sake of the gospel.

Because the wise, the powerful, and the pious of this world continue to reject You, You turn to the weak, the blind, the lame, and the humble, inviting them to eat bread at Your table. Make me one of these who understand they don't deserve the feast You offer. No effort on my part changes this. You wouldn't have suffered and died in my place if it weren't necessary.

I cannot imagine the alternative if Your grace was not offered. Compel me to come to the Dinner. I can never repay You. But I do thank You. In reverence and humility, I accept Your grace. Amen.

1. Look down, O Lord, from heaven behold,
    And let thy pity waken!
    How few the flock within thy fold,
    Neglected and forsaken!
    Almost thou'lt seek for faith in vain,
    And those who should thy truth maintain
    Thy Word from us have taken.
    (Luther 1884k)

* * *

16. Learn from this, then, that our neighbor is to be sought as a lost sheep, that his shame is to be covered with our honor, that our piety is to be a cover for his sins. But nowadays, when men come together they backbite one another; and thus they would show how zealous they are against sin. Therefore, ye men, whenever ye come together, do not backbite your neighbors. Make not one face at one person and another at someone else.... Likewise, ye women, when you come together, conceal the shame of others, and do not cause wounds which you cannot heal. Should you meet with anything like this in some one's house, then throw your mantle over shame and wounds, and close the door. A very good reason for doing this is, that you would have others do, the same to you. (Vol. 4:64)

* * *

Prayer for Luke 15:1–10
The Parable of the Lost Sheep and Lost Coin

Now the tax collectors and "sinners" were all gathering around to hear him. But the Pharisees and the teachers of the law muttered, "This man welcomes sinners and eats with them."

Then Jesus told them this parable: "Suppose one of you has a hundred sheep and loses one of them. Does he not leave the ninety-nine in the open country and go after the lost sheep until he finds it? And when he finds it, he joyfully puts it on his shoulders and goes home. Then he calls his friends and neighbors together and says, 'Rejoice with me; I have found my lost sheep.' I tell you that in the same way there will be more rejoicing in heaven over one sinner who repents than over ninety-nine righteous persons who do not need to repent.

"Or suppose a woman has ten silver coins and loses one. Does she not light a lamp, sweep the house and search carefully until she finds it? And when she finds it, she calls her friends and neighbors together and says, 'Rejoice with me; I have found my lost coin.' In the same way, I tell you, there is rejoicing in the presence of the angels of God over one sinner who repents." (NIV, 1984)

Seeker of the Lost,

You don't look down Your nose at me when I wander from the straight and narrow path of righteousness. Forgive me when I am critical of others who stray, for we all fall short of the standards set forth in Scripture. Help me to recognize that You don't turn away from anyone. You seek a relationship with every person. Increase my awareness that the more I turn away from sinners, the more I distance myself from Your example.

When some point to Scriptures that say "avoid the wicked and put away evil," guide me to focus on Your perfect example. Help me resist wielding the laws of Moses or the institutional church to embarrass or demean others. The Law is no one's lord. You alone are the Lord. You took the sin of the world upon Yourself and covered our faults with Your good example. Teach me to do the same with others. Let me stand between sinners and their accusers.

Teach me to find my place among outcasts of the community where I will do more good as their defender than I will as one who condemns them. I'll never understand why You love them if I don't get close to them. As I befriend others, may my love for You and my efforts to live decently be a positive influence. Open me up to the possibility that I may gain as much from the interaction as they do.

It's hard for me to swallow that my piousness might be a greater sin than the low living of some people. Yet I admit that religious practices enhance my sense of goodness and lead me to despise the sin I see in others. Forgive me for reducing the heights and depths of my own errors.

I acknowledge and confess my sin before You, O Lord. I am as lost as the next person when I'm not walking humbly with You. Show me that You are eager to comfort and bring peace to those who fear they cannot do enough to cover their sins. Let me feel joy like the angels when anyone hears Your Word and accepts the freedom found in You.

You are the Good Shepherd. When I look to You, I never fear condemnation for having been lost, but I rejoice in the safety, protection, and peace You freely offer. Pick me up and carry me on Your shoulders. Give me such security that I do not resist Your aid. I delight that You found me. Now I have Your example to instruct me better than any law could teach me. Grace and mercy are mine. Guide me to live a life that is pleasing to You. Amen.

1. Though in midst of life we be,
    Snares of death surround us;
    Where shall we for succor flee,
    Lest our foes confound us?
    To thee alone, our Saviour.
    We mourn our grievous sin which hath
    Stirr'd the fire of thy fierce wrath.
    Holy and gracious God! Holy and mighty God!
    Holy and all-merciful Saviour!
    Thou eternal God!
    Save us, Lord, from sinking
    In the deep and bitter flood.
    Kyrie eleison. [Lord have mercy.]
    (Luther 1884u)

* * *

3. St. Paul says, I Tim. 6:10: "The love of money is the root of all kinds of evil," whence cometh strife, pride, war and bloodshed. Therefore it is also called here the unrighteous mammon, because it is applied to such evil uses, and is a great cause of evil to men. 4. Nevertheless it is God's creature like wine and corn, and the creatures of God are good. Why then does he call them evil? Because they tempt us to so much evil… And thus, since mammon runs into the service of evil, Christ calls it mammon of unrighteousness, namely, that which we have above our needs and we will not use in helping our neighbor; for this we possess unrighteously, and before God it is stolen goods, for in the presence of God one is bound to give and lend, and suffer himself to be deprived of it." (Vol. 4:293-4)

* * *

Prayer for Luke 16:1–9
The Parable of the Shrewd Manager

He also said to His disciples: "There was a certain rich man who had a steward, and an accusation was brought to him that this man was wasting his goods. So he called him and said to him, "What is this I hear about you? Give an account of your stewardship, for you can no longer be steward.'

"Then the steward said within himself, "What shall I do? For my master is taking the stewardship away from me. I cannot dig; I am ashamed to beg. I have resolved what to do, that when I am put out of the stewardship, they may receive me into their houses.'

"So he called every one of his master's debtors to him, and said to the first, "How much do you owe my master?' And he said, "A hundred measures of oil.' So he said to him, "Take your bill, and sit down quickly and write fifty.' Then he said to another, "And how much do you owe?' So he said, "A hundred measures of wheat.' And he said to him, "Take your bill, and write eighty.' So the master commended the unjust steward because he had dealt shrewdly. For the sons of this world are more shrewd in their generation than the sons of light.

"And I say to you, make friends for yourselves by unrighteous mammon, that when you fail, they may receive you into an everlasting home." (NKJV)

Bountiful Provider,

You graciously supply more than I need to support my life. Yet it is difficult for me to give from my abundance to those who are poor and needy. Forgive me for the improper ways I use possessions when I serve only my selfishness and pride.

The people of this world know how to get what they want by whatever means they can. Why am I, as Your follower, not as wise as they are? Stir me to seek life through You with the same intensity the people of the world devote to their personal well-being. Lead me to a greater trust in You that brings new life.

Some think by this story You are suggesting good works will help us get into heaven. But a tree must be good before it can yield good fruit. Lord, I have tried to become good on my own effort. I attend church as much as I think is necessary. I'm not sure this is what makes a person pleasing to You, although peer pressure does help me do some things I might not do on my own initiative. Fill me with Your precious Word that teaches me the depths of the grace of God. Make me into a good tree so no one is required to prod me to carry out acts of goodness and love.

I pray that You will change me on the inside so that my actions are motivated by love for You. I long for greater trust in You that brings new life and makes me a new person. I want to be the kind of Christian who seeks opportunities to put my faith into action through acts of love. Confirm that when I help my neighbor, a new life begins to reveal itself, eternal life in You.

Encourage me that the friends I make on earth, those who will receive me into eternal homes, are not the lofty saints whose faith was evident in their good works, but the poor and needy I helped with the overflow of blessings You provided me. I will be grateful to them for giving me the opportunity to feed them when they were hungry and clothe them when they were naked.

Guide me and give me wisdom in gaining the goal I seek in You, eternal life. Grant me faith that cannot keep from producing good works in love. Amen.

3. Thy fold, O God, shall bring to thee
    The praise of holy living;
    Thy word shall richly fruitful be,
    And earth shall yield thanksgiving.
    Bless us, O Father! bless, O Son!
    Grant, Holy Ghost, thy blessing!
    Thee earth shall honor—thee alone,
    Thy fear all souls possessing.
    Now let our hearts say, Amen.
    (Luther 1884n)

* * *

10. So we see now in the example of the rich man that it is impossible to love, where no faith exists, and impossible to believe, where there is no love; for both will and must be together, so that a believer loves everybody and serves everybody; but an unbeliever at heart is an enemy of everybody and wishes to be served by every person, and yet he covers all such horrible, perverted sins with the little show of his hypocritical works as with a sheep's skin; just as that large bird, the ostrich, which is so stupid that when it sticks its head into a bush, it thinks its entire body is concealed. Yea, here you see that there is nothing blinder and more unmerciful than unbelief. For here the dogs, the most irascible animals, are more merciful to poor Lazarus than this rich man, and they recognize the need of the poor man and lick his sores; while the obdurate, blinded hypocrite is so hard hearted that he does not wish him to have the crumbs that fell from his table. (Vol. 4:21–22)

* * *

Prayer for Luke 16:19–31
The Rich Man and Lazarus

"There was a certain rich man who was clothed in purple and fine linen and fared sumptuously every day. But there was a certain beggar named Lazarus, full of sores, who was laid at his gate, desiring to be fed with the crumbs which fell from the rich man's table. Moreover the dogs came and licked his sores. So it was that the beggar died, and was carried by the angels to Abraham's bosom. The rich man also died and was buried. And being in torments in Hades, he lifted up his eyes and saw Abraham afar off, and Lazarus in his bosom.

"Then he cried and said, 'Father Abraham, have mercy on me, and send Lazarus that he may dip the tip of his finger in water and cool my tongue; for I am tormented in this flame.' But Abraham said, 'Son, remember that in your lifetime you received your good things, and likewise Lazarus evil things; but now he is comforted and you are tormented. And besides all this, between us and you there is a great gulf fixed, so that those who want to pass from here to you cannot, nor can those from there pass to us.'

"Then he said, 'I beg you therefore, father, that you would send him to my father's house, for I have five brothers, that he may testify to them, lest they also come to this place of torment.' Abraham said to him, 'They have Moses and the prophets; let them hear them.' And he said, 'No, father Abraham; but if one goes to them from the dead, they will repent.' But he said to him, 'If they do not hear Moses and the prophets, neither will they be persuaded though one rise from the dead.'" (NKJV)

Promise of Abraham,

You always teach about faith and love. I pray, dear Lord, that I will not be like the rich man who takes pride in his outward appearances like keeping the Law and performing holy acts. Remove the spirit from me that cares only for myself, trusts in superficial displays, finds joy only in serving myself, and yields no fruit of love.

I want a trust in You that seeks You above everything else. When You bless me with material goods in excess of my needs, do not let me become entangled in their grasp, but lead me to use them to glorify You in love. Open my eyes to the misery of others that convinces me of the goodness You have showered upon me and draws me to a compassionate response.

Where there is no love, there is no faith. Awaken me to understand that my religious position, credentials, or displays of religious deeds do nothing to deserve Your blessing. Forgive me for the lack of mercy I have shown to the poor and needy.

I don't understand how suffering, poverty, or misery can be a good thing for anyone. To have faith doesn't mean I must suffer, but any state of physical health can teach me to see goodness in You. When I am weak or in pain, give me confidence in Your ability to hear and answer my plea for help. Increase my desire to serve others, even if my physical abilities prevent it. Guide me to see that You place the poor and needy in my doorway as hidden treasures.

Your Word holds people of faith close to You just like Abraham held Lazarus to himself. May I too rest in the comfort of Your Word until the Day of Judgment. I will hold tightly to Your Word that keeps my conscience from terrorizing me and stealing Your peace.

Although it's not wrong, You have not taught or commanded us to pray for the dead. I cannot improve their circumstances. They are in Your eternal care. Let me not rely on departed spirits for knowledge, but on You and Your teaching. You have given me everything I need. Lead me to life. Amen.

3. Rejoice ye, then, that through his Son
   God is with sinners now at one;
   Made like yourselves of flesh and blood,
   Your brother is th' eternal Good.

4. What harm can sin and death then do?
   The true God now abides with you:
   Let hell and Satan chide and chafe,
   God is your fellow-ye are safe.
   (Luther 1884w)

* * *

81. This Gospel sufficiently teaches and represents the entire Christian life with all its events and sufferings; for the two chief things are faith and love. Faith receives the good; love gives the good. Faith offers us God as our own; love gives us to our neighbor as his own. Now when such life begins, God goes to work and improves it by trials and conflicts, through which a man increases more and more in faith and love, that through his own experience God becomes to him so heartily dear and precious, and he no longer fears anything. (Vol. 5:100)

* * *

Prayer for Luke 17:11–19
Jesus Cleanses Ten Lepers

On the way to Jerusalem Jesus was going through the region between Samaria and Galilee. As he entered a village, ten lepers approached him. Keeping their distance, they called out, saying, "Jesus, Master, have mercy on us!" When he saw them, he said to them, "Go and show yourselves to the priests." And as they went, they were made clean. Then one of them, when he saw that he was healed, turned back, praising God with a loud voice. He prostrated himself at Jesus' feet and thanked him. And he was a Samaritan. Then Jesus asked, "Were not ten made clean? But the other nine, where are they? Was none of them found to return and give praise to God except this foreigner?" Then he said to him, "Get up and go on your way; your faith has made you well." (NRSV)

Gift of Love,

Hear me as I cry out to You, O Lord. I have heard of Your goodness. Yet I hesitate to come near You. You are holy and people say I am unclean because of sin. Yet I long to feel connected. I'm tired of people holding me at arm's length. You know my need, even before I ask. Teach me to be more like You so that the love I give in good works will benefit my neighbor.

O Christ, You sent the lepers on their way to the religious establishment, but not because the pious could do anything more to help. Healing came before they could examine the outcasts with their hallowed rules. Let me not be swayed by religious leaders who teach that the Law is the truth of God, who say that to go against the Law is to go against God. They make Your wrath my master. Protect my faith from such teaching.

I may be labeled a renegade by traditionalists, yet in my baptism I vowed to follow You and Your teaching, not human doctrine. Give me trust in You as a God of love and goodness alone.

How do You do it? Your love is so great that You give it knowing the vast majority will be ungrateful. And still, You let them enjoy Your love and kindness. Please guard me from ingratitude and entitlement that cannot understand Your power and grace. Shield me against letting sin, human doctrine, laws, saints, or devils lure me away from You. Give me the strength and conviction to follow my conscience rather than to follow the crowd, even if I'm the only one who returns to You.

You have shown that faith is a journey that does not stop once it has begun. Shield me from the deception that taking a few steps in the journey is enough for salvation. I want a trust in You that is enduring and that will sustain me for the long run. Teach me, guide me, and draw me to greater knowledge of You in study and prayer so that when trials press against me, I will not fall away, but my faith will grow and be strengthened.

Fill me with so much gratitude that I return to You, praising You with a loud voice. May I offer to You all I possess, for I have not brought such blessings upon myself. My greatest reward is to taste and experience the sweetness of You. I will confess and proclaim Your goodness in all the world, for my joy and my life are found in You. Help me in faith, to receive the good You offer, and in love, to share Your goodness with my neighbors. Amen.

2. Th' eternal Father's only Son
   For a manger leaves his throne.
   Disguised in our poor flesh and blood
   See now the everlasting Good.
   Hallelujah!

7. All this he did to show his grace
   To our poor and sinful race;
   For this let Christendom adore
   And praise his name for evermore.
   Hallelujah!
   (Luther 1884a)

* * *

22. Now he comes and praises himself that he is just. He has a poisonous, wicked heart, who praises himself most gloriously on account of his pretended good works, how he fasted and gave the tenth of all he had. Hence he is so full of hatred to his neighbor, if God allowed him to judge, he would plunge the poor publican down into the deepest hell. Behold, is not this a wicked heart and terrible to hear, that I would all men should go to ruin, if only I be praised? Yet all this is so finely decorated and adorned by external conduct, that no one can censure it. Here we see how we are to know the tree from its fruits. For when I view his heart with spiritual eyes, I recognize it is full of blasphemy and hatred to his neighbor. From these fruits I know that the tree is evil. (Vol. 4:346)

* * *

Prayer for Luke 18:9–14
Parable of the Pharisee and Tax Collector

And He also told this parable to some people who trusted in themselves that they were righteous, and viewed others with contempt: "Two men went up into the temple to pray, one a Pharisee and the other a tax collector. The Pharisee stood and was praying this to himself: 'God, I thank You that I am not like other people: swindlers, unjust, adulterers, or even like this tax collector. I fast twice a week; I pay tithes of all that I get.' But the tax collector, standing some distance away, was even unwilling to lift up his eyes to heaven, but was beating his breast, saying, 'God, be merciful to me, the sinner!' I tell you, this man went to his house justified rather than the other; for everyone who exalts himself will be humbled, but he who humbles himself will be exalted." (NASB)

Merciful Savior,

I am easily deceived by outer appearances. Too often, I deceive myself. I use external means to make myself look good. I do the right things for my own good more than for the good of others. Look into my heart and expose my self-serving motivations so that I can see when I'm seeking honor and praise for myself. O God, be merciful to me, a sinner.

I'm deliberate about going to church. I try to obey the commandments. I do my share of good works. This is what I've been taught I'm supposed to do. As exemplary as I think my actions might be, convict my soul with the knowledge of my true heart and my inability to judge anyone else's heart. Lead me to develop a compassionate outlook that seeks the well-being of every person who seeks Your help.

You said that no person is better than another. You find nothing good in the person who thinks he is good. The Law condemns us all and makes us equals before God. I'm afraid I will always have the Pharisee in me. I repeatedly think my external religious practices make me better than those who don't work as hard at it as I do. Help me recognize that when I exalt myself and despise my neighbors, my sin is greater than theirs and I break every commandment.

Change me, Lord, so I stop condemning others for their sins and feeling justified when adversity comes to them. Bring me to the place where I lift them to You in prayer, asking for Your help on their behalf, that they might experience Your comfort too.

Be merciful to me, O God, and free me from my sin. Lead me away from being judgmental. Forgive me for trusting that following rules makes me a good person in Your eyes. Comfort me with Your grace.

Although sin will always bring consequences in this earthly kingdom, You reign in the spiritual kingdom. Fill my heart with Your grace that changes me and encourages me to share myself and Your love with sinners. O God, be merciful to me, a sinner like everyone else. Amen.

9. Bear not false witness, nor belie
   Thy neighbor by foul calumny [slander];
   Defend his innocence from blame,
   With charity hide his shame.
   Have mercy, Lord.

12. Help us, Lord Jesus Christ, for we
    A Mediator have in thee;
    Without thy help our works so vain
    Merit naught but endless pain.
    Have mercy, Lord.
    (Luther 1884t)

* * *

20. This blind man represents the spiritually blind, the state of every man born of Adam, who neither sees nor knows the kingdom of God; but it is of grace that he feels and knows his blindness and would gladly be delivered from it. They are saintly sinners who feel their faults and sigh for grace. But he sits by the wayside and begs, that is, he sits among the teachers of the law and desires help; but it is begging, with works he must appear blue and help himself. (Vol. 2:131)

* * *

Prayer for Luke 18:31–43
A Blind Man Recognizes the Messiah

Then [Jesus] took the twelve aside and said to them, "See, we are going up to Jerusalem, and everything that is written about the Son of Man by the prophets will be accomplished. For he will be handed over to the Gentiles; and he will be mocked and insulted and spat upon. After they have flogged him, they will kill him, and on the third day he will rise again." But they understood nothing about all these things; in fact, what he said was hidden from them, and they did not grasp what was said.

As he approached Jericho, a blind man was sitting by the roadside begging. When he heard a crowd going by, he asked what was happening. They told him, "Jesus of Nazareth is passing by." Then he shouted, "Jesus, Son of David, have mercy on me!" Those who were in front sternly ordered him to be quiet; but he shouted even more loudly, "Son of David, have mercy on me!" Jesus stood still and ordered the man to be brought to him; and when he came near, he asked him, "What do you want me to do for you?" He said, "Lord, let me see again." Jesus said to him, "Receive your sight; your faith has saved you." Immediately he regained his sight and followed him, glorifying God; and all the people, when they saw it, praised God.
(NRSV)

Healer of the Blind,

Why did You so willingly offer Yourself as a sacrifice for my sin? I have heard of Your great kindness; You experienced dreadful pain and suffering on my behalf. I've also heard that the prophets, the angels, and even You foretold all of this. There is so much I don't understand. Nevertheless, I thank You for so great a sacrifice.

Reason tells me good works should help to gain Your favor, yet my efforts blind me to the magnitude of both my sin and Your grace. Shield me from those who would convince me that I must also suffer in some way, mentally, physically, personally, to atone for my sin or to be worthy of Your salvation. Your suffering alone has accomplished everything. I confess I get confused with varying religious interpretations and often I don't know which way to turn. Heal me, Lord, for I am blind, and I want to see.

I come to You, Jesus, because others have told me You are gentle and compassionate. They say You desire to help those who call on You. Some people may not think I'm worthy of Your attention because I haven't done as much as they have done, but still I cry out to You. Hear me, O Christ. Save me from my blindness and my sin. Guide me to persist through all obstacles until You hear me and open my eyes to see all truth is found in You. Let my humble prayers be as incense to You and my childlike trust in Your goodness as the fragrance of honeysuckle.

For too long, I have believed teachers of the Law who tell me everything I must do to help myself. They are the blind trying to lead the blind. Give me no fear of the gospel even if it changes my concept of religion and reveals how little I understand. Free me from dependence on rules and human doctrines. In Your lovingkindness, O Christ, grant me trust in You alone.

As I begin to comprehend the magnitude of Your goodness and grace, teach me to walk in Your example, the way of love and sacrificial service for the good of all people. I will honor You with my life. I will praise You with my life. I will serve You with my life. I will forever offer You the sacrifice of praise and thanksgiving. Amen.

1. Christ, who freed our souls from danger,
   And hath turned away God's anger,
   Suffered pains no tongue can tell,
   To redeem us from pains of hell.

5. Trust God's Word; it is intended
   For the sick who would be mended;
   Those whose heavy-laden breast
   Groans with sin, and is seeking rest.
   (Huss 1884)

* * *

21. Is it not a thing most abominable, that God who feeds so many mouths, should be held in such low esteem by me, that I will not trust him to feed me? Yea, that a guilder, thirty-eight cents, should be valued more highly than God, who pours out his treasures everywhere in rich profusion. For the world is full of God and his works. He is everywhere present with his gifts, and yet we will not trust in him, nor accept his visitation. Shame on thee, thou cursed world! What kind of a child is that, who cannot trust in God for a single day, but trusts in a guilder? (Vol. 4:325)

* * *

Prayer for Luke 19:41–48
Jesus Weeps over Jerusalem

As he approached Jerusalem and saw the city, he wept over it and said, "If you, even you, had only known on this day what would bring you peace—but now it is hidden from your eyes. The days will come upon you when your enemies will build an embankment against you and encircle you and hem you in on every side. They will dash you to the ground, you and the children within your walls. They will not leave one stone on another, because you did not recognize the time of God's coming to you."

Then he entered the temple area and began driving out those who were selling. "It is written," he said to them, "'My house will be a house of prayer'; but you have made it 'a den of robbers.'"

Every day he was teaching at the temple. But the chief priests, the teachers of the law and the leaders among the people were trying to kill him. Yet they could not find any way to do it, because all the people hung on his words. (NIV, 1984)

Compassionate Lord,

If I only took time to consider how You continue to watch and weep over Your people, I might begin to grasp that we are so poor and blind to Your riches, lost in the comforts of the moment. I want to embrace the peace You want for me. Make me aware of Your help and counsel so I recognize the dangers that surround me.

The nation of Israel claimed it was chosen by God, in possession of a promised tract of land, the temple, and the God they believed to dwell in it. I fool myself if I think this is an image of security. Yes, things can appear calm for a few moments, but guard me from trusting in beautiful buildings and financial assets that can be demolished and lost overnight. Let me grasp this biblical event, not merely as a historical occurrence, but as a reflection of my homeland.

The gospel is the treasure by which we are persuaded to follow God's will. Keep us from disregarding its enormous value lest we find everything falling in around us. Awaken us from our apathy, O Lord. I cannot fully comprehend the power of Your Word to change my life. Let it open my heart to understand the grace You showed in coming as a man to serve us, to die and rise from the dead, to send the Holy Spirit, to give us Your Word, and to open heaven wide for all to enter.

When an entire nation minimizes Your Word, they are headed for big trouble. Hear my prayer that all nations will recognize and seek the kind of peace You want, and keep us all from believing that contentment lies in the possessions of this world. Teach me that pennies in my pockets cannot give me more courage than You who hold heaven and earth. Build a house of prayer within me where I can learn to depend on You alone and where You can dwell.

Make me wary of churches that turn Your house into a marketplace, preaching for money, robbing souls of true life, and selling forgiveness for money or good works. Send the power of Your Word to diminish their influence. Please reign among us, O Christ, and multiply Your people.

Send wise and compassionate ministers so that those who have not heard the Word may find peace in You. Cleanse us of false worship, priests, and people so that only You remain as Lord of the temple and we can praise God for abundant grace and mercy. Amen.

1. Wilt thou, O man, live happily,
   And dwell with God eternally,
   The ten commandments keep, for thus
   Our God himself biddeth us.
   Kyr' eleison!

2. I am the Lord and God! take heed
   No other god doth thee mislead;
   Thy heart shall trust alone in me,
   My kingdom then thou shalt be.
   Kyr' eleison!
   (Luther 1884z)

* * *

18. "Distress of nations [confused]" does not refer to the body... I take it that it is the condition of agonized conscience. For since the Gospel, by which alone the troubled conscience can be comforted, is condemned, and in its stead there are set up doctrines of men, which teach us to lay aside sin and earn heaven by works; there must come a burdened and distressed conscience, a conscience that can find no rest, that would be pious, do good and be saved, that torments itself and yet does not know how to find satisfaction. Sin and conscience oppress, and however much is done no rest is found. By these the sinner becomes so distressed that he knows not what to do nor whither to flee. Hence arise so many vows and pilgrimages and worship of the saints and chapters for mass and vigils. (Vol. 1:67–68)

* * *

Prayer for Luke 21:25–36
The Coming of the Son of Man

[Jesus said,] "There will be signs in the sun, the moon, and the stars, and on the earth distress among nations confused by the roaring of the sea and the waves. People will faint from fear and foreboding of what is coming upon the world, for the powers of the heavens will be shaken. Then they will see 'the Son of Man coming in a cloud' with power and great glory. Now when these things begin to take place, stand up and raise your heads, because your redemption is drawing near."

Then he told them a parable: "Look at the fig tree and all the trees; as soon as they sprout leaves you can see for yourselves and know that summer is already near. So also, when you see these things taking place, you know that the kingdom of God is near. Truly I tell you, this generation will not pass away until all things have taken place. Heaven and earth will pass away, but my words will not pass away. Be on guard so that your hearts are not weighed down with dissipation and drunkenness and the worries of this life, and that day does not catch you unexpectedly, like a trap. For it will come upon all who live on the face of the whole earth. Be alert at all times, praying that you may have the strength to escape all these things that will take place, and to stand before the Son of Man." (NRSV)

Guardian of my Soul,

I am deeply concerned about the state of affairs in the world today. I don't see how things can get any worse. Why do so few people seem to care that the Day of Judgment might be near? You told us there would be signs of the coming of Your kingdom, but every generation thinks things have never been more dire.

Even religious institutions have fallen into grievous error. When religious leaders focus on everything except You, O Christ, it's like

You are covered with a cloud. Help me to cling to You alone as the Light who reveals the love and goodness of God.

The Church becomes like the darkened moon when it stops reflecting You, the source of light. Keep me from relying on the example of the Church when it gets caught up in worshiping obedience to rules and mandatory morality. Help me instead to focus on actions of love that reflect You.

Assure me that I don't need to follow Christian leaders whose own importance and outward displays of piety have surpassed their passion for You. They are like falling stars in the night. Lead me never to think religious position, authority, or good works bring salvation. Build my trust in You alone, for You have removed the burden of my sin.

Fear is a common motivator in the practice of religion. I question if I've done enough to win Your favor at the time I will stand before You. Give me the peace of knowing I can do nothing except trust that You have done all that is necessary to secure my eternal future. Cleanse me from self-centered living and let Your perfect love within me cast out fear. Assured that a season of growth is a sure sign of Your coming, lead me to yield the fruit of faith.

As we, Your people, wait for You to return, give us joy that makes us sing, knowing You are coming to redeem us and to grant us the crown of life. Deliver us from all evil. Fill us with the blessed hope of Your return in glory.

Let the Holy Scriptures, a tree of life, blossom with hope and guidance and faith. Empower Your Word to bring growth in me. Remove from me the desire to sin, and teach me to live in holiness and righteousness. Come, Lord Jesus. Let Your kingdom break forth in me today. Amen.

3. Thy kingdom come! Thine let it be
   In time, and through eternity!
   O let thy Holy Spirit dwell
   With us, to rule and guide us well;
   From Satan's mighty power and rage
   Preserve thy Church from age to age.
   (Luther 1884q)

* * *

12. It is, therefore, his purpose to teach us by this narrative, given for our instruction and consolation, how his work is to be done in the Christian church after his resurrection, namely, that he will not reject nor cast out those who are weak in their faith, yea, not even those who are held in error or ignorance, or who are otherwise weak, fearful, and despairing. They are rather the very persons in whom he will exercise and manifest the power of his resurrection, not only by inviting them to come to him, but also by coming to them, and treating them in the gentlest and kindest way, talking with them, teaching and instructing them, yea, even eating with them, until at length they grow strong and secure in their faith; while their hearts, so sad and sorrowful for a time, are again filled with joy. (Vol. 2:288)

* * *

Prayer for Luke 24:13–35
The Walk to Emmaus

Now behold, two of them were traveling that same day to a village called Emmaus, which was seven miles from Jerusalem. And they talked together of all these things which had happened. So it was, while they conversed and reasoned, that Jesus Himself drew near and went with them. But their eyes were restrained, so that they did not know Him.

And He said to them, "What kind of conversation is this that you have with one another as you walk and are sad?"

Then the one whose name was Cleopas answered and said to Him, "Are You the only stranger in Jerusalem, and have You not known the things which happened there in these days?"

And He said to them, "What things?"

So they said to Him, "The things concerning Jesus of Nazareth, who was a Prophet mighty in deed and word before God and all the people, and how the chief priests and our rulers delivered Him to be condemned to death, and crucified Him. But we were hoping that it was He who was going to redeem Israel. Indeed, besides all this, today is the third day since these things happened. Yes, and certain women of our company, who arrived at the tomb early, astonished us. When they did not find His body, they came saying that they had also seen a vision of angels who said He was alive. And certain of those who were with us went to the tomb and found it just as the women had said; but Him they did not see."

Then He said to them, "O foolish ones, and slow of heart to believe in all that the prophets have spoken! Ought not the Christ to have suffered these things and to enter into His glory?" And beginning at Moses and all the Prophets, He expounded to them in all the Scriptures the things concerning Himself.

Then they drew near to the village where they were going, and He indicated that He would have gone farther. But they constrained Him, saying, "Abide with us, for it is toward evening, and the day is far spent." And He went in to stay with them.

Now it came to pass, as He sat at the table with them, that He took bread, blessed and broke it, and gave it to them. Then their eyes were opened and they knew Him; and He vanished from their sight.

And they said to one another, "Did not our heart burn within us while He talked with us on the road, and while He opened the Scriptures to us?" So they rose up that very hour and returned to Jerusalem, and found the eleven and those who were with them gathered together, saying, "The Lord is risen indeed, and has appeared to Simon!" And they told about the things that had happened on the road, and how He was known to them in the breaking of bread. (NKJV)

Risen Lord,

Some of Your followers don't believe it was necessary for You to rise from the grave; they reject Your resurrection. This is the same thing as not knowing or recognizing You. Fill me with absolute trust in Your resurrection because it displays the most convincing evidence of who You are—the Son of God.

Some stories people tell of how they have experienced Your presence or teaching are almost impossible to believe. I don't want to be so blinded by skepticism that I can't see You in my own life. Open my mind to accept the witness of the apostles in the gospels. Your presence and power are seen today. Draw closer to us, dear Jesus. We need You. Bring power to the stories we have heard of You. Only You can use the resurrection to kindle our spirits and make us fruitful.

Forgive me, Lord, if I have belittled Your work by trying to make it understandable. It's just that Your work is too exalted—greater than the human mind can grasp. Just because I have read the Bible doesn't mean I understand it. The stories themselves have no power to teach the truth. You are the Word who teaches me. Be present with me when I study the Scriptures and teach me how to listen for Your voice.

When I waver in my faith, come to me and renew my strength. Remove fear and weakness of faith from me so I can believe Your Word. In Your mercy, be patient with me. Cause my heart to burn with desire to know more about You. I want to eat and drink with You so I can know You better. Having created this desire in me, do not refuse to give Yourself to me. I need the assurance only You can give, and that's why I come to the sacrament.

Help the Church to mimic Your actions, for in doing so it becomes Your Body on earth. O Christ, You accepted the weak in faith, the ignorant, and those who were wrong in their thinking to eat with You. It was to these You manifested the power of Your resurrection. You revealed Yourself to the women first and they proclaimed the grandest work of God—the resurrection. Forgive us when we assume we know who is or isn't worthy to sit at Your table or proclaim Your presence among us. Give us patience to work with those who stumble and err in their actions. Show us how to use our gifts and powers to serve all people, to instruct, console, reprove, and offer kindness until they grow and become strong.

I have read and heard the witnesses of Your death and resurrection. I will trust this happened according to God's perfect plan. Give me simplicity of heart and the faith of a child, and then in my rejoicing, lead me to bear fruit for You. Amen.

1. Christ was laid in Death's strong bands
    For our transgressions givén.
    Risen, at God's right hand he stands
    And brings us life from heavén.
    Therefore let us joyful be
    Praising God right thankfully
    With loud songs of Hallelujah!
    Hallelujah!
    (Luther 1884b)

* * *

22. He shows them his hands and his feet, and comforts them, saying: "Why are ye troubled? and wherefore do questionings arise in your hearts? See my hands and my feet, that it is I myself: handle me and see; for a spirit has not flesh and bones," etc.

23. This is nothing but a sermon that teaches us not to be offended in the weak Christ. He does not rebuke the disciples harshly, does not say: Away with you; I do not want you. You should be strong and courageous, but here you sit and are dismayed and terrified! He does not do these things; but lovingly comforts them, that he might make them strong and fearless, and not only this but also cheerful and of good courage. Therefore we ought not to cast away the weak, but so deal with them that, from day to day, we may bring them to a condition that they may become strong and of good cheer. (Vol. 2:311–312)

* * *

Prayer for Luke 24:36–47
The Ascension of Jesus

While they were talking about this, Jesus himself stood among them and said to them, "Peace be with you." They were startled and terrified, and thought that they were seeing a ghost. He said to them, "Why are you frightened, and why do doubts arise in your hearts? Look at my hands and my feet; see that it is I myself. Touch me and see; for a ghost does not have flesh and bones as you see that I have." And when he had said this, he showed them his hands and his feet. While in their joy they were disbelieving and still wondering, he said to them, "Have you anything here to eat?" They gave him a piece of broiled fish, and he took it and ate in their presence. Then he said to them, "These are my words that I spoke to you while I was still with you—that everything written about me in the law of Moses, the prophets, and the psalms must be fulfilled." Then he opened their minds to understand the scriptures, and he said to them, "Thus it is written, that the Messiah is to suffer and to rise from the dead on the third day, and that repentance and forgiveness of sins is to be proclaimed in his name to all nations, beginning from Jerusalem."
(NRSV)

Forgiver and Redeemer,

I don't blame people for wanting to see You as a strong, commanding Savior, one whose power crushes the enemy. Many find it difficult to follow or trust in a helpless man on a cross. Make me different. I want to recognize You and not fear when You appear in a form I don't understand. Guard me from thinking that if You are in me I will possess power to do mighty deeds. Help me realize that when I do things that appear weak to others, this is often where You are most present.

Comfort me and grant Your peace to me. Expose the tricks of the evil one who makes us think we must do more to help ourselves and always leaves us troubled. When I see weakened and fearful

Christians, let me see You in them. In the same way Your skin was pierced and torn, prevent me from hiding my own painful wounds, but to encourage others by sharing my own life experience. Inspire me to help and support them until they become strengthened in their faith, fearless in their trust in You.

In Your precious name, the sins of the whole world have been swallowed up. Let all who trust this know the joy, assurance, and comfort it gives. Remove the veil from my eyes that conceals a weak and sinful nature, and let me taste the sweetness of Your forgiveness. Call me to true repentance, which turns away from sin and reforms my whole life. Stop me when I start to think self-chastisement does anything to blot out sin.

Bind the gospel message to my heart. I want to hold tightly to the forgiveness that is mine. Bring gladness and eager obedience so I am encouraged to do the things I should.

I trust You have forgiven all the sin of my past, present, and future. Ward off any temptation to increase in sin because I know of Your grace. Give me wisdom to recognize that new sin always brings negative consequences. When I fear for my eternal well-being, remind me that all of my sins were nailed to the cross with You. Open Your hands and Your feet that I may observe the wounds You received for my sake, and grant that I may experience both comfort and regret.

Just as You directed your disciples to Scripture to strengthen and confirm their faith, guide me in Your Word to find the assurance I need. Amen.

5. To the Father whence he came
   He returns with brighter fame;
   Down to hell he goes alone,
   Then ascends to God's high throne.

6. Thou, the Father's equal, win
   Victory in the flesh o'er sin;
   So shall man, though weak and frail;
   By the indwelling God prevail.
   (Ambrose 1884)

* * *

15. The word of man may also in this connection be used in a measure as an illustration; for by it the human heart is known. Thus we commonly say: I understand his heart or intentions, when we have only heard his words; as out of the fullness of the heart the mouth speaks, and from the word the heart is known....With this also corresponds the gospel of Matthew 12, 34, where Christ says: "Out of the abundance of the heart the mouth speaketh...." The bird is known by its song, for it sings according to its nature. Therefore all the world knows that nothing represents the condition of the heart so perfectly and so positively as the words of the mouth, just as though the heart were in the word.

16. ...But here in God, the Word does not only carry with it the sign and picture, but the whole being, and is as full of God as he whose word or picture it is. (Vol. 1:178–179)

* * *

Prayer for John 1:1–14
Jesus is the Living Word

In the beginning was the Word, and the Word was with God, and the Word was God. He was in the beginning with God. All things were made through Him, and without Him nothing was made that was made. In Him was life, and the life was the light of men. And the light shines in the darkness, and the darkness did not comprehend it.

There was a man sent from God, whose name was John. This man came for a witness, to bear witness of the Light, that all through him might believe. He was not that Light, but was sent to bear witness of that Light. That was the true Light which gives light to every man coming into the world.

He was in the world, and the world was made through Him, and the world did not know Him. He came to His own, and His own did not receive Him. But as many as received Him, to them He gave the right to become children of God, to those who believe in His name: who were born, not of blood, nor of the will of the flesh, nor of the will of man, but of God.

And the Word became flesh and dwelt among us, and we beheld His glory, the glory as of the only begotten of the Father, full of grace and truth. (NKJV)

Merciful and Blessed Christ,

You became fully human, fulfilling the prophecy and promise of the Old Testament. This is my belief. You are the living Word through whom God speaks and reveals the Godhead. Open my mind to understand that You convey the exact nature and heart of God.

You lived Your life according to the wisdom of the eternal God. As I seek to experience life as You intended, set me free of my dependence on human reasoning and help me to follow Your example of humility and service.

I accept You as the light that shows God's grace to the world. When the Law shines its light and exposes my sinfulness, I cringe in shame. Still I resist. I try to follow what human leaders have told me I should do, but then I am placing more trust in church doctrines than I am in Your example. I have not yet learned to bask in Your light, which reveals the path to the abundant life. Free me from all distractions and guide me to live in the good news. Bless me with faith that clings only to You.

John the Baptist came pointing to You to prepare the world for the revelation of God's true nature. Like John, let me point to You as tangible evidence that our God is merciful and full of grace. Instill in me the conviction that You alone make the Godhead known. Fill me with this certainty so I can cast out any human teaching that gets in the way of God's disclosure in You.

Nowhere do the Gospels say I have to understand everything about them to believe. I wouldn't need faith if I understood everything. The light of truth is seen only by faith. Bless me with trust in You that is so strong and sure that it overcomes my need to comprehend all things before I am willing to give my life to You. Help me realize that nothing I do of my own effort, reason, or free will can achieve what Your grace has already done.

My greatest wish, dear Lord, is to know You are the true gift, the Messiah, who displays the image of God. In this faith, craft me as Your child. Let Your light beam the true nature of God into my soul. What good news it is to see God in Christ alone! I praise Your holy and loving name. Amen.

5. These are the tokens ye shall mark,
   The swaddling-clothes and manger dark;
   There shall ye find the young child laid,
   By whom the heavens and earth were made.

6. Now let us all, with gladsome cheer,
   Follow the shepherds, and draw near
   To see this wondrous gift of God,
   Who hath his own dear Son bestowed.
   (Luther 1884f)

* * *

52. "But in order that you may not also despair of God, behold, I will show you how to get rid of your sins and obtain salvation. Not that you can strip off your sins or make yourselves pious through your works; another man is needed for this; nor can I do it, I can point him out, however. It is Jesus Christ, the Lamb of God. He, he, and no one else either in heaven or on earth takes our sins upon himself. You yourself could not pay for the very smallest of sins. He alone must take upon himself not alone your sins, but the sins of the world, and not some sins, but all the sins of the world, be they great or small, many or few." This then is preaching and, hearing the pure Gospel, and recognizing the finger of John, who points out to you Christ, the Lamb of God. (Vol. 1:132)

* * *

Prayer for John 1:19–28
The Testimony of John the Baptist

This is the testimony given by John when the Jews sent priests and Levites from Jerusalem to ask him, "Who are you?" He confessed and did not deny it, but confessed, "I am not the Messiah." And they asked him, "What then? Are you Elijah?" He said, "I am not." "Are you the prophet?" He answered, "No." Then they said to him, "Who are you? Let us have an answer for those who sent us. What do you say about yourself?" He said,
   "I am the voice of one crying out in the wilderness,
   'Make straight the way of the Lord,'"
   as the prophet Isaiah said.
Now they had been sent from the Pharisees. They asked him, "Why then are you baptizing if you are neither the Messiah, nor Elijah, nor the prophet?" John answered them, "I baptize with water. Among you stands one whom you do not know, the one who is coming after me; I am not worthy to untie the thong of his sandal." This took place in Bethany across the Jordan where John was baptizing. (NRSV)

Present and Indwelling Christ,

The state of religion is so political and vain. People seek fame and influence for their own advantage. They want others to look up to them. They take sides. Let me be content to endorse You alone. Just as John refused to be glorified, so let me direct all glory to You, whose sandals I am unworthy to untie.

John the Baptizer did not come as a prophet to tell of a future messiah. He pointed to You, a present day Messiah. Wake me up and show me that You are here. You are now. You are the Anointed One living among us today. Let me shout: "Salvation has come!" because You live and reign today.

The Hebrew for "make straight" is literally "turn and do." I wish I could always obey the commands of God, but I can't. My nature is sinful. Turn me. I really do want to walk in Your ways, which are love, mercy, goodness, and compassion. I cannot do these things of my own will. Saying prayers, attending church, and doing committee work makes me feel righteous, but truthfully, only You can be the love, mercy, and goodness that comes out of me.

O God, Your Law is the most perfect way. Although it instructs me toward life, it gives no power to live according to it. When I examine the Law, what I see is my inability to keep it. Be merciful to me, a sinner, O Lord. I cannot save myself. When I hear that You have taken my sins upon Yourself, draw me to believe You are the gospel and all I need for salvation. Come, Lord Jesus; remove sin from my life. Then give me confidence to speak the good news I know in You, especially the news of the cross.

Ease the burden I place on myself when I think I must earn divine favor with my own efforts. Forgive me for imagining I need to make myself worthy of receiving God's mercy. You gave Your life to rescue me. Instill trust in me that what You did for all the world got the job done.

You are the Lamb who took my sin and the sin of the entire world upon Yourself. Blessed be the Lamb of God. I want to please You in everything I do and say. I cannot become a better person without You. Please live and reign in me forever. Amen.

1. To Jordan came our Lord the Christ,
   To do God's pleasure willing,
   And there was by Saint John baptized,
   All righteousness fulfilling;
   There did he consecrate a bath
   To wash away transgression,
   And quench the bitterness of death
   By his own blood and passion;
   He would a new life give us.
   (Luther 1884v)

* * *

18. Hence the highest thought in this Gospel lesson, and it must ever be kept in mind, is, that we honor God as being good and gracious, even if he acts and speaks otherwise, and all our understanding and feeling be otherwise. For in this way feeling is killed, and the old man perishes, so that nothing but faith in God's goodness remains, and no feeling. For here you see how his mother retains a free faith and holds it forth as an example to us. She is certain that he will be gracious, although she does not feel it. She is certain also that she feels otherwise than she believes. Therefore she freely leaves and commends all to his goodness, and fixes for him neither time nor place, neither manner nor measure, neither person nor name. He is to act when it pleases him. (Vol. 2:63)

* * *

Prayer for John 2:1–11
The Wedding in Cana

On the third day a wedding took place at Cana in Galilee. Jesus' mother was there, and Jesus and his disciples had also been invited to the wedding. When the wine was gone, Jesus' mother said to him, "They have no more wine."

"Dear woman, why do you involve me?" Jesus replied. "My time has not yet come."

His mother said to the servants, "Do whatever he tells you."

Nearby stood six stone water jars, the kind used by the Jews for ceremonial washing, each holding from twenty to thirty gallons.

Jesus said to the servants, "Fill the jars with water"; so they filled them to the brim. Then he told them, "Now draw some out and take it to the master of the banquet."

They did so, and the master of the banquet tasted the water that had been turned into wine. He did not realize where it had come from, though the servants who had drawn the water knew. Then he called the bridegroom aside and said, "Everyone brings out the choice wine first and then the cheaper wine after the guests have had too much to drink; but you have saved the best till now."

This, the first of his miraculous signs, Jesus performed at Cana in Galilee. He thus revealed his glory, and his disciples put their faith in him. (NIV, 1984)

Giver of New Wine,

You instituted marriage to cultivate and exercise trust within human relationships. You bonded me to Yourself in the same kind of personal and passionate relationship through baptism. May You, the Word, be invited into every marriage, spiritual and carnal, to bless and sweeten the promises made.

In the course of life's celebration, the source of gladness is depleted. Often, Christ, I do not seek Your help until all hope is gone and I realize I cannot provide for all my needs from my own resources. Humble me, Lord, so I am willing to ask for Your help and can live a life of joy in relationship with You.

Sometimes I feel like Mary when she asked for Your help. You turned away without helping. Yet when it appears You are rejecting my requests, teach me to trust completely in Your goodness and in Your ability to provide what is needed. Give me patience to wait for Your timing, for I know Your wisdom is far greater than my understanding. Grant me the good sense to tell others to do as You say rather than to rely on human interpretation and doctrine that overload Your teaching.

Water in stone jars for ritual purification is like the Law in my hardened heart. Help me to grasp that I cannot purify myself through efforts to be obedient, no matter how intensely I try. Turn me so I trust in You to transform me rather than in following laws that only purify a person to a small degree on the outside. You have fulfilled the Law. You took my sins upon Yourself and cleansed me. Now I can appreciate the Law for its guidance and protection. I can delight in it. It's sweeter than honey.

Thank You, O Christ, that I no longer need to fulfill the Law's demands to change my outward actions. I want to drink Your desires into my soul so Your will becomes a natural part of who I am.

O God, Your goodness, mercy, and wisdom are incomprehensible. Your instruction is my joy and Your will has been made known in the Son. Fill me with complete trust in Your power to rescue me every time I fail to follow Your will. Amen.

3. To show us this, he hath his word
   With signs and symbols given;
   On Jordan's banks was plainly heard
   The Father's voice from heaven:
   "This is my well-beloved Son,
   In whom my soul delighteth;
   Hear him." Yea, hear him every one
   Whom he himself inviteth,
   Hear and obey his teaching.
   (Luther 1884v)

* * *

13. Now, the beginning of this birth was in baptism. The water is baptism; the Spirit is that grace which is given to us in baptism. The result of this birth is clearly seen in the hour of death or in times of test by poverty and temptation. He who is born of the flesh fights to defend himself, looks hither and thither, employs his reason to make his living. But he who is born anew reasons thus: I am in God's hands, who has preserved and nourished me before in a wonderful manner; he will also feed and preserve me in the future and save me from all sorrow and misfortune. (Vol. 3:415)

* * *

Prayer for John 3:1–15
Nicodemus Visits Jesus

Now there was a Pharisee named Nicodemus, a leader of the Jews. He came to Jesus by night and said to him, "Rabbi, we know that you are a teacher who has come from God; for no one can do these signs that you do apart from the presence of God." Jesus answered him, "Very truly, I tell you, no one can see the kingdom of God without being born from above." Nicodemus said to him, "How can anyone be born after having grown old? Can one enter a second time into the mother's womb and be born?" Jesus answered, "Very truly, I tell you, no one can enter the kingdom of God without being born of water and Spirit. What is born of the flesh is flesh, and what is born of the Spirit is spirit. Do not be astonished that I said to you, 'You must be born from above.' The wind blows where it chooses, and you hear the sound of it, but you do not know where it comes from or where it goes. So it is with everyone who is born of the Spirit." Nicodemus said to him, "How can these things be?" Jesus answered him, "Are you a teacher of Israel, and yet you do not understand these things?

"Very truly, I tell you, we speak of what we know and testify to what we have seen; yet you do not receive our testimony. If I have told you about earthly things and you do not believe, how can you believe if I tell you about heavenly things? No one has ascended into heaven except the one who descended from heaven, the Son of Man. And just as Moses lifted up the serpent in the wilderness, so must the Son of Man be lifted up, that whoever believes in him may have eternal life."
(NRSV)

Beloved Teacher,

The ways of the Spirit are hard to comprehend. Conflicting religious explanations don't make it any easier. Like Nicodemus, I want to understand how to secure my eternal future, and reason tells me to work harder. But if I could understand it all, I wouldn't need faith. I will simply trust that my new birth began when I was baptized, when I received this sacramental sign of Your grace and the Spirit began to work in me through the water and the Word.

Some intellectual teachers think they can explain spiritual matters by reading words on the pages of Scripture. Nicodemus was well educated. He interpreted Your words literally and they didn't make sense. Forgive and heal my blindness when I think human reason can explain the mind of God.

Reason cannot answer all the questions in the natural world, yet I foolishly expect it to explain the spiritual world. My soul is in Your hands, O Lord. Let my desire be to comprehend only what You know I am ready to learn. I want to become the person You intended, living the quality of life You want for me.

I'm not sure how to become a different person from how I was made in the beginning. I try my best to be a good person. And then I sin. It doesn't seem like I gain any ground. But You say it's not up to me. I can't do anything in my own power to get into the kingdom of God. It doesn't make sense that I can't help. Yet if I could help, maybe I'd just take the credit for some of the progress. Help me in this struggle. Forgive me for thinking Your grace is dependent on me and what I do.

Whenever the Word is preached, that You received the wrath of God in my place, caress my ears as if that physical sound is the Spirit bringing music to my ears. How inconceivable that You would do such a thing for me! I want to believe it. It's just that I know I deserve to be condemned. Give me peace in trusting You satisfied my punishment. Free me to live my life unconstrained by rules and teachings of others that are born only of reason.

By the Spirit, teach me to offer what You want of me—my heart, my soul, my full confidence in Your saving sacrifice on the cross. Amen.

3. O holiest Fire! O Source of rest!
   Grant that with joy and hope possest,
   And in thy service kept forever,
   Naught us from thee may sever.
   Lord, may thy power prepare each heart;
   To our weak nature strength impart,
   Onward to press, our foes defying,
   To thee, through living and through dying.
   Hallelujah! Hallelujah!
   (Luther 1884d)

* * *

20. Therefore, this gift—all of grace—is much greater, transcends and is mightier, than all the sins on earth, so that the unworthiness of any man, yes of all men together, aye the eternal wrath and condemnation which they have deserved, cannot be so great that the greatness of this love and grace, or forgiveness, does not in every particular outweigh, yes, engulf them; as Paul says, Rom. 5:20: "But where sin abounded, grace abounded more exceedingly;" and Ps. 103:11, 12: "For as the heavens are high above the earth.... so far hath he removed our transgressions from us." (Vol. 3:357)

* * *

Prayer for John 3:16–21
God's Love for the World

"For God so loved the world that He gave His only begotten Son, that whoever believes in Him should not perish but have everlasting life. For God did not send His Son into the world to condemn the world, but that the world through Him might be saved.

"He who believes in Him is not condemned; but he who does not believe is condemned already, because he has not believed in the name of the only begotten Son of God. And this is the condemnation, that the light has come into the world, and men loved darkness rather than light, because their deeds were evil. For everyone practicing evil hates the light and does not come to the light, lest his deeds should be exposed. But he who does the truth comes to the light, that his deeds may be clearly seen, that they have been done in God." (NKJV)

Compassionate Gift of the Father,

In You alone I recognize the good news. You reveal the Father to the world as a loving, overflowing fountain of grace. Banish any lingering fear I may possess that understands the Father as a demanding taskmaster. Grant me enduring peace in knowing I am no longer condemned for my sins. I am forgiven.

Help me, O Christ, to see You as the Mediator between the world and God. When I reject You, I expose myself to the consequences of sin. And still, You are my refuge. May I always trust in Your sacrifice for me and in the Father's incomprehensible love, which provided You as the doorway to eternal life.

Only the love and grace of God could save the world, for God did not send You to judge the world but to be its Savior. Bring to an end any thoughts I have of You as my judge, for this only brings fear of what You could rightfully do to me because I am still sinful. Show me that my salvation lies in trusting You are my best friend who came to take sin, death, and hell away. A friend would not hold these over me.

Send Your Spirit and make me a new person. Teach me to love the light. Support me in trusting that Your light is God's love for the world. Build up in me, O Christ, a faith in You that defeats fear of an angry God and clings to You alone as my salvation. Guide me to live my life the way You lived Your life, for the sake of others. Inspire me to live for the good of my neighbor.

I cannot comprehend the love of a God who would give such a precious gift as an only Son to a hateful and hostile world. Thank You, Father, for giving us the gift that is all in all. How much more evidence do I need that You would not withhold anything good from those who place their faith in You?

Joy, love, peace, hope, goodness, kindness, and eternal life will not be withheld from those who love and trust in Christ. Open my eyes wide to see the Father through You. Teach me to receive every blessing that comes from trusting in You. Amen.

1. May God be prais'd henceforth and blest forever!
   Who, himself both gift and giver,
   With his own flesh and blood our souls doth nourish;
   May they grow thereby and flourish!
   Kyri' eleison!
   By thy holy body, Lord, the same
   Which from thine own mother Mary came,
   By the drops thou didst bleed,
   Help us in the hour of need!
   Kyri' eleison!

2. Thou hast to death thy holy body given,
   Life to win for us in heaven;
   By stronger love, dear Lord, thou couldst not bind us,
   Whereof this should well remind us.
   Kyri' eleison!
   Lord, thy love constrain'd thee for our good
   Mighty things to do by thy dear blood;
   Thou hast paid all we owed,
   Thou hast made our peace with God.
   Kyri' eleison.
   (Luther 1884m)

* * *

4. Thus we, read in the Gospel, that, although the disciples of Christ without doubt believed (for otherwise they had not followed him), yet he often rebuked them on account of their weak faith. They had indeed faith, but when it was put to the test, they let it sink and did not support it. So it is with all Christians; where faith is not continually kept in motion and exercised, it weakens and decreases, so that it must indeed vanish; and yet we do not see nor feel this weakness ourselves, except in times of need and temptation, when unbelief rages too strongly; and yet for that very reason faith must have temptations in which it may battle and grow. (Vol. 5:254)

* * *

Prayer for John 4:46–54
Jesus Heals the Official's Son

Then [Jesus] came again to Cana in Galilee where he had changed the water into wine. Now there was a royal official whose son lay ill in Capernaum. When he heard that Jesus had come from Judea to Galilee, he went and begged him to come down and heal his son, for he was at the point of death. Then Jesus said to him, "Unless you see signs and wonders you will not believe." The official said to him, "Sir, come down before my little boy dies." Jesus said to him, "Go; your son will live." The man believed the word that Jesus spoke to him and started on his way. As he was going down, his slaves met him and told him that his child was alive. So he asked them the hour when he began to recover, and they said to him, "Yesterday at one in the afternoon the fever left him." The father realized that this was the hour when Jesus had said to him, "Your son will live." So he himself believed, along with his whole household.

Now this was the second sign that Jesus did after coming from Judea to Galilee. (NRSV)

Author of my Faith,

I'm afraid I don't understand much about faith even though I have believed in You for a long time. Sometimes I think I'm so strong that nothing will shake my faith. Then I'm tested—and I fail You. Yet it is through trials that You provide the opportunity to exercise trust in You and Your Word. Give me confidence to follow what You taught so I can witness You fulfilling Your promises every time.

When I first heard and believed the good news for myself, I assumed this was all I needed. Yet faith is a living thing and growing confidence in You is as important as the beginning of faith. Build up the treasure of Your gospel in me, a brittle earthen vessel. I feel so weak and fragile in the storms of life. While I feel certain about some things, I know I cannot face life's struggles without You. Help me or I am lost.

It's one thing to believe You can help a person when they see You visibly, but I want to learn how to trust You even when I cannot sense Your presence. I find it easy to trust in You when things are going well. But forgive me for acting like You are no longer gracious and good as soon as I have a bad day. When temptations push against my faith, guide me to grasp You and Your promises more firmly, for this will bring me to a new level of understanding of Your goodness.

As my heart and mind are opened, let me see the image of God as it has been revealed in You, and my faith will be transformed from one degree of glory to another. I cannot fathom Your goodness all at once. I can only submit to let You lead me, one step at a time, as only You can.

Merciful God, You invited me to become a Christian. Help me to follow the example of Christ and to increase in faith daily. Even if the whole world should fall and each person conspire to do evil and the devil break all earthen vessels, yet I will not be turned.

• With Your divine help, I will abide in the gospel. Bring my understanding of You to the point where I cannot keep such good news to myself, for the greatest work of faith is sharing You with others. Amen.

5. The silver seven times tried is pure
   From all adulteration;
   So, through God's word, shall men endure
   Each trial and temptation:
   Its worth gleams brighter through the cross,
   And, purified from human dross,
   It shines through every nation.
   (Luther 1884k)

* * *

1. In today's Gospel Christ gives us another lesson in faith, that we should not be overanxious about our daily bread and our temporal existence, and stirs us up by means of a miracle; as though to say by his act what he says by his words in Matthew 6,33: "Seek ye first the Kingdom of God, and his righteousness, and all these things shall be added unto you." For here we see, since the people followed Christ for the sake of God's Word and the signs, and thus sought the Kingdom of God, he did not forsake them but richly fed them. He hereby also shows that, rather than those who seek the Kingdom of God should suffer need, the grass in the desert would become wheat, or a crumb of bread would be turned into a thousand loaves. (Vol. 2:167)

* * *

Prayer for John 6:1–15
Feeding the Five Thousand

After these things Jesus went over the Sea of Galilee, which is the Sea of Tiberias. Then a great multitude followed Him, because they saw His signs which He performed on those who were diseased. And Jesus went up on the mountain, and there He sat with His disciples.

Now the Passover, a feast of the Jews, was near. Then Jesus lifted up His eyes, and seeing a great multitude coming toward Him, He said to Philip, "Where shall we buy bread, that these may eat?" But this He said to test him, for He Himself knew what He would do.

Philip answered Him, "Two hundred denarii worth of bread is not sufficient for them, that every one of them may have a little."

One of His disciples, Andrew, Simon Peter's brother, said to Him, "There is a lad here who has five barley loaves and two small fish, but what are they among so many?"

Then Jesus said, "Make the people sit down." Now there was much grass in the place. So the men sat down, in number about five thousand. And Jesus took the loaves, and when He had given thanks He distributed them to the disciples, and the disciples to those sitting down; and likewise of the fish, as much as they wanted. So when they were filled, He said to His disciples, "Gather up the fragments that remain, so that nothing is lost." Therefore they gathered them up, and filled twelve baskets with the fragments of the five barley loaves which were left over by those who had eaten. Then those men, when they had seen the sign that Jesus did, said, "This is truly the Prophet who is to come into the world."

Therefore when Jesus perceived that they were about to come and take Him by force to make Him king, He departed again to the mountain by Himself alone. (NKJV)

Bread of Heaven,

You richly feed all who follow You and who seek the kingdom of God. This includes not only the pious, but the weak as well. Heighten my awareness of Your concern for me, and for all people, as shown in the signs You perform and as heard in the message of Your goodness.

Sometimes I'm embarrassed I have so little to give to advance Your purposes through the Church. Assure me that nothing I offer is too small or insignificant for You to bless and to increase for the benefit of others. Teach me to be frugal, preserving Your gifts and not letting Your blessings go to waste. There will always be great needs and Your provision is sure. We need more than food for the body. In You, O Christ, there is nourishment for the soul.

Grass possesses little nourishment to humans. When I trust in outward righteousness by working to appear holy and wise, I deceive myself and think I am flourishing like the grass. Yet You have seen how quickly my righteousness fades. I need to receive and rely on Your Spirit more than my own effort. I hunger to be filled and satisfied with the Word rather than with any religious works I perform.

You come into me through my physical senses. As I hear and read the stories in Scripture, nourish my soul. When I imagine the example of the patriarchs, prophets, and apostles, arouse in me the love and trust they displayed. May I regularly receive You, the Word, so I can pass You along to others who hunger to be fed.

There are so many people who are hungry for the bread You offer. Open my eyes to readily share the witness of the apostles that have been gathered together in the New Testament. They pointed to You for life. You pointed to my neighbor as the one I should love as the evidence of my love for God. Because it takes two for love to exist, inspire me to bring love into existence.

Direct me to the Scriptures when I too need a word of life. Guide me, good Lord, to never doubt Your ability to change me and others with the message of grace in You. Only through You will I find deliverance, satisfaction, peace, and joy. Assure me that You don't require I be without possessions to serve You well, yet give me a heart that is content with little and a spirit that trusts You will provide. Amen.

3. Him thou hast unto all set forth,
   Their great salvation,
   And to his kingdom called the earth-
   Every nation.
   By thy dear, health-giving word,
   In every land resounding.

4. He is the Health and blessed Light
   Of lands benighted,
   By him are they who dwelt in night
   Fed and lighted.
   While his Israel's hope he is,
   Their joy, reward and glory.
   (Luther 1884i)

* * *

20. What is the proof by which one may know that this heavenly bread is his and that he is invited to such a spiritual supper? He needs only to look at his own heart. If he finds it so disposed that it is softened and cheered by God's promises and is firm in the conviction that it may appropriate this bread of life, then he may be assured that he is one of the invited.... From that moment on, he loves his neighbor and helps him as his brother; he rescues him, gives to him, loans to him and does nothing for him but that which he would desire his neighbor to do for himself. All this is attributable to the fact that Christ's kindness to him has leavened his heart with sweetness and love, so that he has pleasure and joy in serving his neighbor; yea, he is even in misery if he has no one to whom to show kindness. (Vol. 3:403–404)

* * *

Prayer for John 6:44–51
The Bread of Life

[Jesus said,] "No one can come to me unless drawn by the Father who sent me; and I will raise that person up on the last day. It is written in the prophets, 'And they shall all be taught by God.' Everyone who has heard and learned from the Father comes to me. Not that anyone has seen the Father except the one who is from God; he has seen the Father. Very truly, I tell you, whoever believes has eternal life. I am the bread of life. Your ancestors ate the manna in the wilderness, and they died. This is the bread that comes down from heaven, so that one may eat of it and not die. I am the living bread that came down from heaven. Whoever eats of this bread will live forever; and the bread that I will give for the life of the world is my flesh." (NRSV)

Food for the World,

Even though the Word tells me I am saved by divine grace through Jesus Christ and my efforts to appease God do nothing to help, I tend to fall back into the mindset that I must work hard if I want to be certain I am saved. *Almighty God, merciful Father, help me now! I cannot help myself. Christ, my Lord, do help now, for with only my own effort, all is lost!** What can I do to be at peace with my eternal end? Please teach me according to Your Word.

If I only knew and understood the truth about God, I would never fear anything again. I would fall helplessly in love and want to please God in all things. Fill me with the knowledge of God as I look at You, O Christ. You are the cornerstone and foundation of my faith. You reveal God in Yourself, as a gracious Savior, a Comforter, and Helper.

My spirit is fed and nourished when I trust in You, knowing that You came in flesh and blood, suffered for my sin and paid the penalty of death. Give me a faith in You that comforts me whenever I'm tempted to think You require anything more than trusting in You. Fill me with the joy of carrying Your yoke, which is easy and sweet, so that I find pleasure in living for You.

Feed me the spiritual bread of heaven in the Word. You are the Word. You are the meal that sustains my famished spirit. Assure me every time I receive the sacrament of Holy Communion that Your body and blood have rescued me from sin and death. You are heavenly bread that fills my soul because the Father's promise in You brings joy to me.

I confess that my heart is not always pure when I help my neighbor. So often the good I attempt is more for my own benefit, often to increase my sense of eternal security. I'm not even sure I know how to help my neighbor purely for his [or her] own benefit. Forgive me for these selfish motives and for thinking I need to help myself as much as I need to trust in You. You alone are the hope the Father has given to draw me away from myself. I want to give my heart and soul, my complete confidence, to You.

Lead me to serve You in my neighbors, to care for them like brothers and sisters. I want to love You in my neighbor and to please You in everything I do. May the works I do be pure. Let them be the evidence that my love for You is true. Amen.

*(Italics: Luther 1983, Vol. 3:396-397)

2. That we never might forget it,
   Take my flesh, he said, and eat it,
   Hidden in this piece of bread,
   Drink my blood in this wine, he said.

4. Praise the Father, God in heavén,
   Who such dainty food hath givén,
   And for misdeeds thou hast done
   Gave to die his belovéd Son.
   (Huss 1884)

* * *

5. In this way Christ teaches us here the fate that awaits us Christians and his Word; both our life and our doctrine must be condemned and reviled, and that by the foremost, wisest and greatest of earth. Thus one knows the corrupt tree by its fruits, as they, under the pretense of being good, are so bitter, angry, impatient, cruel and mad as to condemn and pass sentence, when one touches them at their tender spot and rejects their ideas and ways. (Vol. 2:173)

* * *

Prayer for John 8:46–59

Glorifying the Father Instead of Abraham

[Jesus said,] "Can any of you prove me guilty of sin? If I am telling the truth, why don't you believe me? He who belongs to God hears what God says. The reason you do not hear is that you do not belong to God."

The Jews answered him, "Aren't we right in saying that you are a Samaritan and demon-possessed?"

"I am not possessed by a demon," said Jesus, "but I honor my Father and you dishonor me. I am not seeking glory for myself; but there is one who seeks it, and he is the judge. I tell you the truth, if anyone keeps my word, he will never see death."

At this the Jews exclaimed, "Now we know that you are demon-possessed! Abraham died and so did the prophets, yet you say that if anyone keeps your word, he will never taste death. Are you greater than our father Abraham? He died, and so did the prophets. Who do you think you are?"

Jesus replied, "If I glorify myself, my glory means nothing. My Father, whom you claim as your God, is the one who glorifies me. Though you do not know him, I know him. If I said I did not, I would be a liar like you, but I do know him and keep his word. Your father Abraham rejoiced at the thought of seeing my day; he saw it and was glad."

"You are not yet fifty years old," the Jews said to him, "and you have seen Abraham!"

"I tell you the truth," Jesus answered, "before Abraham was born, I am!" At this, they picked up stones to stone him, but Jesus hid himself, slipping away from the temple grounds. (NIV, 1984)

Revealing Light,

Give me wisdom and patience to pause and reflect on the views of others when they differ from my own. Grant me discernment to recognize and accept the Truth. And give me humility to admit when I am in error. My life is the only evidence that shows others what I believe about You. Guide my actions so they back up the truth I know in You.

Many will scrutinize what I say without hearing the Word I share. Shield me from taking offense at their reactions. Lead me to pray for their healing. Some who criticize me will be very knowledgeable about the Bible. Yet they forget that bitterness, anger, impatience, and a judgmental attitude are fruits of a corrupt tree. Bring peace to me in the midst of criticism, O Christ.

Calm my reactions to people when they throw stones at Your Divine nature. They can't hurt or offend You with their words. You're the Maker of heaven and earth. I'm the one whose beliefs are threatened. Forgive my defensiveness when my views are challenged. Make me so secure in my understanding of You that I don't need to protect You or myself. Help me, O God, to trust that in Your wisdom You remain hidden to some even though they search the Scriptures daily.

Many of our differences arise out of a sincere desire to follow the truth, yet we vary in our interpretations of Scripture. O Christ, You could not be given to every man, woman, or child in Your bodily form. It's only in the gospel that You can be shared with the whole world. Help me understand why I should not place the Law above You, for You are the life-giving Word, and let me consider it a precious gift to share You with others. Not even death can separate us from You when we keep You in our hearts.

Walk with each of Your children through life's difficulties like You walked with Israel through the Red Sea, bringing them safe to the other side. It doesn't matter what others do to my honor and reputation. I will not stop speaking of Your goodness, grace, and lovingkindness. I will always sing of Your glory and honor. Fill me with peace, knowing that Your goodness is sure. Amen.

6. Thy truth thou wilt preserve, O Lord,
   From this vile generation;
   Make us to lean upon thy word,
   With calm anticipation.
   The wicked walk on every side
   When, 'mid thy flock, the vile abide
   In power and exaltation.
   (Luther 1884k)

* * *

12. Remember well that the sheep have to pass judgment upon that which is placed before them. They should say: We have Christ as our Lord and prefer his Word to the words of any man or to those of the angels of darkness.... For Christ says here that the sheep judge and know which is the right voice and which is not. Now let them come along. Have they [the religious leaders] decreed anything? We will examine whether it is right, and according to our own judgment interpret that which is a private affair for each individual Christian, knowing that the authority to do this is not human, but divine. Even the real sheep flee from a stranger and hold to the voice of their shepherd. (Vol. 3:378–379)

* * *

Prayer for John 10:1-11
Jesus the Gatekeeper

[Jesus said,] "Very truly, I tell you, anyone who does not enter the sheepfold by the gate but climbs in by another way is a thief and a bandit. The one who enters by the gate is the shepherd of the sheep. The gatekeeper opens the gate for him, and the sheep hear his voice. He calls his own sheep by name and leads them out. When he has brought out all his own, he goes ahead of them, and the sheep follow him because they know his voice. They will not follow a stranger, but they will run from him because they do not know the voice of strangers." Jesus used this figure of speech with them, but they did not understand what he was saying to them.

So again Jesus said to them, "Very truly, I tell you, I am the gate for the sheep. All who came before me are thieves and bandits; but the sheep did not listen to them. I am the gate. Whoever enters by me will be saved, and will come in and go out and find pasture. The thief comes only to steal and kill and destroy. I came that they may have life, and have it abundantly.

"I am the good shepherd. The good shepherd lays down his life for the sheep." (NRSV)

Good and Only Shepherd,

I am grateful for people who sense the call to enter the office of ministry. You have placed within them the desire to proclaim the Word and to care for Your sheep. Guide those who have been given the authority to approve candidates for ministry to seek direction from the Holy Spirit. Inspire those who are training to be preachers to speak no word other than You and Your teachings.

Restrain ministers from supplementing the Word with human doctrines that set You aside through encouraging reliance on one's own goodness for salvation. Help me to recognize and forsake those preachers who are like thieves and bandits tending the sheep.

I see so many ministers who don't teach You alone. They teach that Christians must perform specific acts displaying outward holiness to get into heaven. Give me confidence to take responsibility for my present and future wellbeing. Guide me to use common sense as I evaluate whether a religious practice is helping me to glorify Your name or promoted as a requirement to reach my heavenly home. Lead me in the way that glorifies You.

Bless those who are true gatekeepers, who use the Law only to reveal how helpless I am to earn Your favor. They open the way to You, the Good Shepherd. Only You can feed me, protect me, care for me, and bring me into joyful pastures. I will follow wherever You lead. Lord, You dwell in those preachers who comfort the flock, who cheer us with voices that relieve our fears and give us liberty. You are not in the voice that creates fear. Open my ears to recognize Your voice in those who console and inspire trust in God.

You call me by name when the special gifts I possess are needed in the work of my church or in service to my neighbor. Increase my love and willingness to respond when help is needed. Now that neither the Law nor sin rule over me, guide me to follow the example You have set.

Feed me with Your Word as daily bread, for it leads me to exercise my faith. I come to You unforced, not strong-armed or shamed, but willingly. Use the Word to draw me and create in me a hunger to know You more completely. Amen.

4. How long, by folly blindly led,
　　Will ye oppress the needy,
　　And eat my people up like bread?
　　So fierce are ye, and greedy!
　　In God they put no trust at all,
　　Nor will on him in trouble call,
　　But be their own providers.

5. Therefore their heart is never still,
　　A falling leaf dismays them;
　　God is with him who doth his will,
　　Who trusts him and obeys him;
　　But ye the poor man's hope despise,
　　And laugh at him, e'en when he cries,
　　That God is his sure comfort.
　　(Luther 1884o)

* * *

14. Christ teaches us in this Gospel to look to him alone as the true shepherd, who only is the founder, lord and head of the church, and says his sheep hear his voice, and not a stranger's. Hereby he indicates that these are the true church, without regard to their being under the pope and his bishops, or even under Moses. For he and his kingdom and church are bound neither to Moses' Law nor to Judaism, although they were instituted by God, much less to the government of pope and bishops, established by themselves. Neither has he taken or received anything from them, but he is the Lord of Moses and of all creatures, to whom all men should be subject. (Vol. 3:50)

* * *

Prayer for John 10:11–16
Jesus the Good Shepherd

[Jesus said,] "I am the good shepherd. The good shepherd gives His life for the sheep. But a hireling, he who is not the shepherd, one who does not own the sheep, sees the wolf coming and leaves the sheep and flees; and the wolf catches the sheep and scatters them. The hireling flees because he is a hireling and does not care about the sheep. I am the good shepherd; and I know My sheep, and am known by My own. As the Father knows Me, even so I know the Father; and I lay down My life for the sheep. And other sheep I have which are not of this fold; them also I must bring, and they will hear My voice; and there will be one flock and one shepherd. (NKJV)

Protecting and Unifying Shepherd,

You are right. I am like a sheep, one of the dumbest of animals—and yet so valuable to You that You laid down Your life for me. To know this insults me and comforts me at the same time. Grant me wisdom to know which leaders are mouthpieces of Your Word. Reassure me that many who lead in the Church truly desire to please You. They are the ones who tenderly care for the sick and weak in the same way You did.

I am a sheep with so many flaws. You know how to encourage me to do what is best for me. You don't beat me with the Law or threaten me with punishment like other shepherds. Thank You for accepting me into Your kingdom.

It's discomforting to listen to shepherds whose preaching makes me think You will only accept strong Christians who are following their rules. They speak for their own profit and to raise an audience for themselves. Train my ears to recognize the consoling sound of Your voice. I want to follow the instruction You offer.

Teach me to be cautious of people, inside or outside the church, who have contempt for compassionate shepherds as well as the sheep. They come as wolves dressed in sheep's clothing. I know You want me to follow the Ten Commandments, yet I pray that You will send pastors who point to You as my refuge because they I know I will fail. Give me wisdom to know my best defense against the devil comes, not because I work hard to follow God's commandments or church doctrines, but because I trust Your protective arms surround me.

O Christ, You alone know Your sheep. End my fear of condemnation by people who scorn placing trust in You ahead of their rules and doctrines. I want to follow You. Forgive me if enthusiasm for my own church denomination makes me think I am a better Christian than others. Make the Word my only authority. Help me to understand Your kingdom is not made up of the high and mighty, but only of the weak, the sick, the infirm, the lowly who gather under Your tender care.

Open my heart and mind to grasp the depths of You. I want to comprehend the treasure of Your death and resurrection. Because You are my Shepherd, I will follow You and Your example. Amen.

4. For this, saith God, I will arise,
   These wolves my flock are rending;
   I've heard my people's bitter sighs
   To heaven my throne ascending:
   Now will I up, and set at rest
   Each weary soul by fraud opprest,
   The poor with might defending.
   (Luther 1884k)

* * *

28. If all the preachers arise and preach the Law, attempting thereby to make people godly, what do they accomplish? They accomplish nothing. For, briefly, there must first be love in the heart, otherwise nothing is accomplished in keeping the Law.... Teach first of all how to obtain love, then men will be able to keep the Law. The Holy Spirit is given, as we have stated, for the purpose of abrogating [formally putting aside] the Law. Hence, Christians are not to be governed by laws.... Now, Christ does not want us to keep his Word with outward observance, like a finite law, but with the heart, with joy and love. But who will give us this joy and love? The Holy Spirit gives it, and no one else. (Vol. 3:283)

* * *

Prayer for John 14:23–31
The Promise of the Holy Spirit

Jesus answered him, "Those who love me will keep my word, and my Father will love them, and we will come to them and make our home with them. Whoever does not love me does not keep my words; and the word that you hear is not mine, but is from the Father who sent me.

"I have said these things to you while I am still with you. But the Advocate, the Holy Spirit, whom the Father will send in my name, will teach you everything, and remind you of all that I have said to you. Peace I leave with you; my peace I give to you. I do not give to you as the world gives. Do not let your hearts be troubled, and do not let them be afraid. You heard me say to you, 'I am going away, and I am coming to you.' If you loved me, you would rejoice that I am going to the Father, because the Father is greater than I. And now I have told you this before it occurs, so that when it does occur, you may believe. I will no longer talk much with you, for the ruler of this world is coming. He has no power over me; but I do as the Father has commanded me, so that the world may know that I love the Father. Rise, let us be on our way." (NRSV)

New Law of my Heart,

I stand in the dark among dead people who follow the Law of Moses as the foundation of their religion, and they follow it with unwillingly hearts. This law-abiding religion can never give life to any soul. It inspires more fear of my Creator than love or good works. Let Your Holy Spirit fall upon me with such authority that a mighty peace fills me and gives me courage and confidence. I want to testify to the love of God, which I've seen in You. Implant a spirit of devotion for God in my heart, for this is what motivates me to be obedient to God's will.

O Spirit of Christ, You are the one who opens my heart to understand the Father is not angry with me, but is kind and gracious. Comfort and relieve me of any lingering fear of my heavenly Father. Thank You that You did not add more laws to my burden. Instead, You have released me from them and set me free to love.

I get upset with myself when I act in ways that dishonor Your will. I don't know why I do things I know are not loving. Help me. Replace my attraction to things of this world with greater love for God because love alone fulfills the Law. I want the knowledge of You that changes me on the inside and makes me want to do what is good and right.

Holy Spirit, guide me by the law of love You have written in my heart so I can serve with joy. When I fail and use my freedom in ways that harm others, confirm my need for Christ and His help. Instill in me such confidence in God's grace and mercy that I am eager to share the Father's goodness, revealed in and through the Son.

Lord, it's hard for me to understand how You bring peace in turbulent times. I want the trouble or affliction removed, but You change the heart to know how to deal with it. Teach me to see the joy and consolation that can be found in life's difficulties. You are able to turn everything into good. Encourage me that I'm always learning, never perfect, in a constant state of development in this life. Create in me the desire to trust in You with all my heart and stir my love for You to go beyond words to acts of caring for my neighbor. Amen.

3. Holy Spirit, with us stay,
　　Nor suffer us to perish;
　　All our sins O take away,
　　Us dying, cheer and cherish.
　　From the power of hell defend;
　　This grace to us be granted:—
　　Upon thee to be planted,
　　In heartfelt faith undaunted,
　　Trusting thee unto the end;
　　With saints of every nation,
　　Escaping hell's temptation,
　　Kept by the Lord's salvation.
　　Amen! Amen! Answer send!
　　So sing we all Hallelujah!
　　(Luther 1884g)

* * *

3. By faith, everything falls that reason can or ever has devised for the salvation of the soul. It must chastise the apish tricks of the whole world, and its jewel alone must be praised. The world cannot endure this, therefore it rushes in, destroys, kills, and says: 'It is expedient for you that one man should die for the people, and that the whole nation perish not,' as Caiaphas says in Jn 11, 50. Thus, the confession must break forth, that God alone is the Saviour; and the same confession brings us into danger of losing our lives. As the Lord says later to the disciples: 'They shall put you out of the synagogues.' (Vol. 3:246)

* * *

Prayer for John 15:26–16:4
Persecution for Following Christ

[Jesus said,] "When the Helper comes, whom I will send to you from the Father, that is the Spirit of truth who proceeds from the Father, He will testify about Me, and you will testify also, because you have been with Me from the beginning. These things I have spoken to you so that you may be kept from stumbling. They will make you outcasts from the synagogue, but an hour is coming for everyone who kills you to think that he is offering service to God. These things they will do because they have not known the Father or Me. But these things I have spoken to you, so that when their hour comes, you may remember that I told you of them. These things I did not say to you at the beginning, because I was with you." (NASB)

Guardian and Stronghold,

I could not know the truth without the Holy Spirit to teach me about You and the Father. You and the Father are one. Keep me from trusting the worldview that is guided only by human reason and cannot see or know You. I have witnessed Your goodness and presence in my life. Let me never fail to share with others how You are my comfort, my strength, and my salvation.

The religious establishment has portrayed a demanding Father for centuries and that conflicts with what You reveal about the Father. How can I turn away from holy tradition? Give me courage to walk the path that Scripture opens to me, O Christ, for Your teachings and human teachings cannot stand together.

You alone are the foundation of faith. Draw me to You as the gospel that human institutions cannot accept. It would be nice if sharing the gospel resulted in welcome. But the gospel will always bring opposition from those who don't know God. Give me courage to trust that You alone accomplished everything needed for the redemption of the world, a gift from heart of the Father.

It's confusing when it's not only the world that persecutes Your disciples for sharing the truth about You, it's also the leaders of the institutional church authorized to teach, baptize, administer sacraments, absolve, and ordain. They think they are defending God's will in defending what they do. Uphold me when they dishonor and banish me from their institutions because I confess the truth the Scriptures teach me about You.

I know the gospel can only make sense to those who are taught by the Spirit. I pray that You will open the minds of more people to understand the Father through Yourself. I pray that my testimony will touch the hearts of people You bring into my life so they too will experience You as a gift.

Fill me with the Holy Spirit and empower me to resist uncertainty and restrain sin. Guide me to respect the office of the Church, which You set in place for continuing Your work in the world. We are all imperfect people, capable of being lured back to the Law with its requirements.

I will rest assured that what You did in dying and receiving my sin upon Yourself has secured for me an eternal salvation. What I do from now on makes little different toward that final end, but I pray this comprehension will create such love in my heart that I desire to please You in all things. Amen.

3. For this, my hope in God shall rest,
   Naught building on my merit;
   My heart confides, of him possest,
   His goodness stays my spirit.
   His precious word assureth me;
   My solace, my sure rock is he,
   Whereon my soul abideth.
   (Luther 1884r)

* * *

78. This is truly an incisive text for the article of the three persons in the divine Being, that the Son of God is the Word of the Father in eternity, whom no one hears speak except the Holy Spirit; and he not only hears, but also testifies and proclaims it in the world. And in short, it all tends to this, that it is God's purpose that the Holy Spirit shall teach and pursue only the article of Christ, how we become righteous before God for his sake. (Vol. 3:165)

* * *

Prayer for John 16:5–15
The Work of the Spirit

[Jesus said,] "But now I am going to him who sent me; yet none of you asks me, 'Where are you going?' But because I have said these things to you, sorrow has filled your hearts. Nevertheless I tell you the truth: it is to your advantage that I go away, for if I do not go away, the Advocate will not come to you; but if I go, I will send him to you.

And when he comes, he will prove the world wrong about sin and righteousness and judgment: about sin, because they do not believe in me; about righteousness, because I am going to the Father and you will see me no longer; about judgment, because the ruler of this world has been condemned.

"I still have many things to say to you, but you cannot bear them now. When the Spirit of truth comes, he will guide you into all the truth; for he will not speak on his own, but will speak whatever he hears, and he will declare to you the things that are to come. He will glorify me, because he will take what is mine and declare it to you. All that the Father has is mine. For this reason I said that he will take what is mine and declare it to you." (NRSV)

Teacher of Truth,

How can Your leaving this earth to be with Your Father be to my advantage? I can't do the things You did. I need someone to tell me what to do. Open my eyes and ears to be an attentive student. If You had stayed on earth, I'd be inclined to think Your kingdom is of this world. Just like You did not come to rule on earth, help me see that Your disciples are not sent to dominate the earth but to serve it in love. Teach me about the spiritual kingdom in which You reign today.

Your Word reaches into my heart and soul to examine my motivations, O Christ. You aren't fooled by outward appearances. Lead me away from thinking pious works and holy rituals are the path of salvation. My self-defined righteousness is like a filthy rag. Help me to resist thinking that obeying the commandments is true righteousness. Yet I don't want to live in fear of the Father's wrath, obeying only because I think it will protect me from punishment. I want to trust in Your saving grace, doing all I do because of what You did for me. Guide me in doing the right things because I love You and my neighbor.

Plumb the depths of my heart and inspire me to change my life to imitate the love You showed for the world on the cross. Send Your Holy Spirit to convict me of my real sin—not trusting completely in You. You bled and died to make satisfaction me and for the sin of the world. You didn't fail. Every sin of every person has been washed away. Forgive me for not giving You my whole heart. Give me unshakable confidence that You have accomplished all this for me, and grant me complete assurance that I am free of sin, death, and the devil.

Strengthen me in love so I can resist judging others by external appearance and actions. I am so easily deceived by beautiful practices that may bring more harm than good. Help me remember I am not sent to rule over others in judgment, but only to teach about You and Your ways.

I've tried hard to be good so that I won't appear bad to You, but honestly, I'm tired of trying to force myself to go out of my way to be kind or help people. I want to serve because it brings joy into my life. Let Your resurrection be the new spirit that reigns in me. Use my hands and talents to continue Your work in the world. Help me to serve my neighbor because I know it pleases You and benefits the ones I assist. Amen.

6. Who in this mercy hath not faith,
   Nor aught therein discerneth,
   Is yet in sin, condemned to death,
   And fire that ever burneth;
   His holiness avails him not,
   Nor aught which he is doing;
   His inborn sin brings all to naught,
   And maketh sure his ruin;
   Himself he cannot succor.
   (Luther 1884v)

* * *

21. Christ says here to his disciples, So it will also go with you. The woman is here in such a state of mind that she is fearful of great danger, and yet she knows that the whole work lies in the hands of God; in him she trusts; upon him it is she depends; he also helps her and accomplishes the work, which the whole world could not do, and she thinks of nothing but the time that shall follow, when she shall again rejoice; and her heart feels and says, A dangerous hour is at hand, but afterwards it will be well. Courage and the heart press through all obstacles. Thus it will also be with you, when you are in sorrow and adversity, and when you become new creatures. Only quietly wait and permit God to work. He will accomplish everything without your assistance. (Vol. 3:81)

* * *

Prayer for John 16:16–23
Sorrow Will Turn into Joy

[Jesus said,] "In a little while you will see me no more, and then after a little while you will see me."

Some of his disciples said to one another, "What does he mean by saying, 'In a little while you will see me no more, and then after a little while you will see me,' and 'Because I am going to the Father'?" They kept asking, "What does he mean by 'a little while'? We don't understand what he is saying."

Jesus saw that they wanted to ask him about this, so he said to them, "Are you asking one another what I meant when I said, 'In a little while you will see me no more, and then after a little while you will see me'? I tell you the truth, you will weep and mourn while the world rejoices. You will grieve, but your grief will turn to joy. A woman giving birth to a child has pain because her time has come; but when her baby is born she forgets the anguish because of her joy that a child is born into the world. So with you: Now is your time of grief, but I will see you again and you will rejoice, and no one will take away your joy. In that day you will no longer ask me anything. I tell you the truth, my Father will give you whatever you ask in my name." (NIV, 1984)

Companion and Friend,

Help me understand how being born of the Spirit is a natural but intense process that is not in my hands. I cherish the times when You speak to me through Your Word. Yet sometimes the words on the pages of the Bible don't speak to me and I get concerned. I feel like You have gone away. Grant me patience to wait upon You in confidence, knowing that in a little while, You will return to teach me and bring peace.

Lord, You said I will face trials as one of Your followers. I need You most in difficult circumstances, yet they are the times when You seem to have disappeared. Strengthen my resolve to hold fast to the Word. Reassure me that You will come again soon. Guard me from trusting my feelings concerning Your absence or presence, for my feelings are inconsistent.

I can understand why Your disciples were not strong when You were being taken from them. When I think You have left me, it's almost like experiencing Your death. Strengthen my faith that You always do what You say You will do. Give me wisdom to know God is always at work and accomplishing whatever God wills. You are not dependent on my efforts. Still, I am abundantly blessed when I open my life to let You work through me.

Forgive my weakness when I face perilous circumstances. Refresh me through the knowledge that by going away You were freed from the limitations of a physical body. Now Your immortal Spirit can live and reign in the hearts of all the faithful, and You have no need for food or sleep. Thank You, Jesus, for Your constant presence.

Even though the world finds joy in opposing You, O Christ, grant me joy in Your presence. Even though the world finds joy in silencing Your Word, grant me joy when I take it in. I don't care where they find their joy, only do not depart from me, for that is my greatest sorrow.

Every time You return to me, let me experience Your resurrection anew. Come as my friend and brother in spite of my failings. Bring deep joy and new life when You return, and let all pain and sorrow be forgotten. Every time I face tribulation and temptation, assure me that You will return in a little while. Amen.

4. Our highest comfort in all distress!
   O let naught with fear our hearts oppress:
   Give us strength unfailing O'er fear prevailing,
   When th' accusing foe would overwhelm us.
   Have mercy, Lord.
   (Luther 1884p)

* * *

2. The Lord points out here five things necessary to constitute true prayer. The first is God's promise, which is the chief thing and is the foundation and power of all prayers. For he promises here that it shall be given us if we ask; and besides he swears: "Verily, verily, I say unto you, if ye shall ask anything of the Father, he will give it you in my name." He promises that we might be sure of being heard in prayer; yea, he censures the disciples for the reason that they are lazy and have not therefore been praying. As if he would say: God is ready to give more quickly, and to give more than you ask; yea, he offers his treasures if we only take them. It is truly a great shame and a severe chastisement for us Christians that God should still upbraid us for our slothfulness in prayer, and that we fail to let such a rich and excellent promise incite us to pray. (Vol. 3:168)

* * *

Prayer for John 16:23–30
Jesus Mediates for Us

[Jesus said,] "On that day you will ask nothing of me. Very truly, I tell you, if you ask anything of the Father in my name, he will give it to you. Until now you have not asked for anything in my name. Ask and you will receive, so that your joy may be complete.

"I have said these things to you in figures of speech. The hour is coming when I will no longer speak to you in figures, but will tell you plainly of the Father. On that day you will ask in my name. I do not say to you that I will ask the Father on your behalf; for the Father himself loves you, because you have loved me and have believed that I came from God.

"I came from the Father and have come into the world; again, I am leaving the world and am going to the Father." His disciples said, "Yes, now you are speaking plainly, not in any figure of speech! Now we know that you know all things, and do not need to have anyone question you; by this we believe that you came from God." (NRSV)

Beloved Mediator,

How can I approach the Creator of the universe with the expectation that whatever I ask for in Your name, I will receive? That's like opening a candy store to an undisciplined child. Help me, dear Jesus, to be aware of my selfish inclinations, but even more, to comprehend the goodness of the heavenly Father. Who in his right mind would ignore opening a treasure chest if he believed it possessed such riches? Forgive me for doubting You will hear me. Take away any fear or doubt that weakens my faith, and build my trust in the truth of what You have said. For You are always more ready to give than I am to receive.

Sometimes I am embarrassed to approach You because my sins make me think I don't deserve anything good from You. Then again, when I approach You in arrogance, thinking many and beautiful prayers warrant Your favor, I'm less worthy to receive answers to prayer. Comfort me with knowing You will answer, not because of my good behavior, but because You have promised to.

I'm too quick to pray for things without thinking about what I'm asking for. Guide me when I bring specific concerns to You. Give me the patience to refrain from specifying how each prayer should be answered. Let me trust in the wisdom of Your timing and ways.

Teach me to pray from the depths of my soul. Hear the groaning of the Holy Spirit as my wordless petitions are brought to You. These are the truest prayers. Grant my deepest desires, for You know them before I am aware of them.

Jesus, Your parables are difficult to understand. One of my deepest desires is to understand Your words. I am sincerely grateful to know the Father's boundless love in sending You to remove my sin. Yet You didn't come to earth just because I sinned. You came to make the Father known. Open my mind to comprehend this truth in its entirety.

I want to trust completely in the promises, the love, the mercy, and the truth about God that I see in You. All that I ask, I will ask in Your name, knowing You opened the door to the Father for me. I am sure that I am heard, dear Jesus, not for my sake, but for Your sake and for Your glory. Amen.

1. Out of the deep I cry to thee;
   O Lord God, hear my crying:
   Incline thy gracious ear to me,
   With prayer to thee applying.
   For if thou fix thy searching eye
   On all sin and iniquity,
   Who, Lord, can stand before thee?

2. But love and grace with thee prevail,
   O God, our sins forgiving;
   The holiest deeds can naught avail
   Of all before thee living.
   Before thee none can boast him clear;
   Therefore must each thy judgment fear,
   And live on thy compassion.
   (Luther 1884r)

* * *

35. So we are to give heed to do everything in behalf of our neighbor, and ever to be mindful, that Christ has done this and that for me; why should I not also for his sake freely do all for my neighbor? And see to it that all the works you do, are directed not to God, but to your neighbor. Whoever is a ruler, a prince, a mayor, a judge, let him not think that he is a ruler to gain heaven thereby or to seek his own advantage; but to serve the public. And so with other works, I assume to do for the good of my neighbor....

36. Thus then you have finely portrayed in this Gospel, as in almost all the Gospel lessons these two thoughts, faith and love. Through faith we belong above to God: through love below to our neighbor. That we may thus lay hold of this truth may God give us his help! Amen. (Vol. 2:377)

* * *

Prayer for John 20:19–31
Jesus Appears to His Disciples

Then, the same day at evening, being the first day of the week, when the doors were shut where the disciples were assembled, for fear of the Jews, Jesus came and stood in the midst, and said to them, "Peace be with you." When He had said this, He showed them His hands and His side. Then the disciples were glad when they saw the Lord.

So Jesus said to them again, "Peace to you! As the Father has sent Me, I also send you." And when He had said this, He breathed on them, and said to them, "Receive the Holy Spirit. If you forgive the sins of any, they are forgiven them; if you retain the sins of any, they are retained."

Now Thomas, called the Twin, one of the twelve, was not with them when Jesus came. The other disciples therefore said to him, "We have seen the Lord."

So he said to them, "Unless I see in His hands the print of the nails, and put my finger into the print of the nails, and put my hand into His side, I will not believe."

And after eight days His disciples were again inside, and Thomas with them. Jesus came, the doors being shut, and stood in the midst, and said, "Peace to you!" Then He said to Thomas, "Reach your finger here, and look at My hands; and reach your hand here, and put it into My side. Do not be unbelieving, but believing."

And Thomas answered and said to Him, "My Lord and my God!"

Jesus said to him, "Thomas, because you have seen Me, you have believed. Blessed are those who have not seen and yet have believed."

And truly Jesus did many other signs in the presence of His disciples, which are not written in this book; but these are written that you may believe that Jesus is the Christ, the Son of God, and that believing you may have life in His name. (NKJV)

Forgiving Teacher and King,

There are no barriers that can keep You from coming into my life to reveal Your presence. I have come to know You from the preaching of forgiveness as well from the witness of those You have touched. I am Your disciple. Yet when I don't see You for a couple of days, I forget and become fearful. Lord, strengthen my faith to understand Your abiding presence. Help me to accept that You won't always change the adversity that waits outside the door, but instead, how I perceive and respond to it.

Reassure me that it's not up to me to save myself from sin or death or hell by fasting, or praying much, or performing many good works. Guide me to place my trust in You, for by Your death and resurrection, You offer a peace that endures, even in hardship. I know I see You, Lord, every time I experience the kindness and compassion of human hands fulfilling Your work.

Forgive me when I have been the one who inflicted wounds on people who love me. You gave the Law as an aid to help me recognize when I am hurting others and to remind me of the magnitude of Your mercy. Direct me now to place love as the only law that guides my life.

Because I know I am forgiven, I am filled with joy and gladness. I cannot contain what I know: that You come to rescue sinners like me from fear and sorrow. Just like the Father sent You, send me. I've got my own story to tell about where I've seen You in my life, how I have been healed, and the peace that fills me. In Your resurrection, heaven and earth are mine already. I don't have to worry anymore. What relief, what joy, what peace this brings!

O Christ, breathe Your Holy Spirit upon me. Like Your disciples, grant me the power to forgive those who hurt me. Let me proclaim forgiveness has come in Your name. Lead me to offer forgiveness freely, without cost, the same way You gave it to me.

Thomas was no different from the other ten disciples. They doubted and were afraid until they saw You personally. But You knew those who would come years later would not have the same opportunity. Thank You for the witness of Your disciples who have helped me believe in You. Bless me with the kind of faith that doesn't need to see You to love You and serve You. And point me to my neighbor when I yearn to show my love for You. Amen.

14. My heart for very joy doth leap,
    My lips no more can silence keep,
    I too must sing, with joyful tongue,
    That sweetest ancient cradle song:—

15. Glory to God in highest heaven,
    Who unto man his Son hath given,
    While angels sing, with pious mirth,
    A glad New Year to all the earth.
    (Luther 1884f)

* * *

4. Peter is a type of such wild wanderers; when Christ had commanded him at once to follow him, he turns about and looks after another, worries as to where he is going whom Jesus had loved. Just so these persons do, they let drop what has been commanded them, and look after the lives and works of those God loved, namely his saints; therefore Christ reproves Peter, and says: What is that to thee, where he is wandering? Follow thou me, I will attend to him; how, if I wish him to tarry, wilt thou also tarry? Do you imagine I wish the same from you as from him? No, not so; you attend to your duties. I desire to have many kinds of servants, but not all to be at the same work. (Vol. 1:241)

* * *

Prayer for John 21:19-24
Jesus Redirects Peter's Concern

([Jesus] said this to indicate the kind of death by which he would glorify God.) After this He said to him, "Follow me."

Peter turned and saw the disciple whom Jesus loved following them; he was the one who had reclined next to Jesus at the supper and had said, "Lord, who is it that is going to betray you?" When Peter saw him, he said to Jesus, "Lord, what about him?" Jesus said to him, "If it is my will that he remain until I come, what is that to you? Follow me!" So the rumor spread in the community that this disciple would not die. Yet Jesus did not say to him that he would not die, but, "If it is my will that he remain until I come, what is that to you?"

This is the disciple who is testifying to these things and has written them, and we know that his testimony is true. (NRSV)

Gentle Leader,

What am I to do? When I look around and see what others are doing, I don't know if I'm supposed to follow what they do or if I should do something else. When I see other disciples accomplishing grand things for You, I get overwhelmed. Guide me like You guided David. He wanted to build a temple for the Lord but this work was not given to him and he was stopped. Help me discern what it is You want me to do with the gifts and talents You gave me.

I know You have a plan for me in which I can serve God faithfully and obey the commandments. But it's hard for me to think that I can serve You simply by being a good spouse, parent, child, or laborer. How common! Not to mention boring. Teach me that obedience in these ordinary areas can bring wonderful benefit to others, and You would rather receive this than religious rituals that get in the way of fulfilling these roles. Keep me from laboring to match the accomplishments and efforts of others, and simply use the gifts You gave me with compassion.

When I admire what other faithful servants have done, let me praise You for the work You accomplish through them. Obedience to follow and perform the labor You give us is a higher worship than our actual deeds. Take away my notion that worship of You is only found in the narrow limits of churches, altars, readings, and singings.

I tend to be a little impatient, Lord—maybe even excessively impatient. Forgive me for starting activities thinking my busyness should count for something, and for neglecting work I've considered not important. Grant me peace in waiting for Your word. Then give me a willingness to follow You into the places You call me.

When I don't feel content with what I have or what I'm doing, I imagine others have a better life. Guide me to work less on changing my lot in life, and redirect me to changing my spirit of discontent. Increase my trust in You and Your plan; no one can arrange my life better than You can.

In You, I possess all things. In faith and obedience, bring me rest, peace, and contentment. Even if the world takes everything I have, let my trust in You remain until the last day. Amen.

4. Obedient always, next to me,
   To father and to mother be;
   Kill no man: even anger dread;
   Keep sacred thy marriage-bed.
   Kyr' eleison!

5. Steal not, nor do thy neighbor wrong
   By bearing witness with false tongue;
   Thy neighbor's wife desire thou not,
   Nor grudge him aught he hath got.
   Kyr' eleison!
   (Luther 1884z)

* * *

15. There you will find the divine, good father heart, and, as Christ says, be thus drawn to the Father through Christ. Then will you understand the saying of Christ in John 3, 16: "God so loved the world that he gave his only begotten Son," etc. That means to know God aright, if we apprehend him not by his power and wisdom, which terrify us, but by his goodness and love; there our faith and confidence can then stand immovable and man is truly thus born anew in God. (Vol. 2:190)

* * *

A Prayer for Good Friday—
How to Contemplate Christ's Sufferings

Suffering Lord,

On this day of judgment, O Christ, You took my place. It does me no good to blame others for what was done to You. And I can't just go through the motions of meditating on Your sacrifice, thinking I benefit by doing so. Free my spirit to weep for myself and what I personally have done to inflict this pain on You. Why would the eternal wisdom of God established in You, the Son, ask You to suffer such agony for me? Give me courage to consider the depths of this question.

I have shown disdain for You by the way I have lived the life You breathed into me. The works of my hands drove the nails into Your hands. My wicked thoughts pressed the thorny crown into Your holy brow. Forgive me for the contempt I have shown. I have been living in false security and ignorance. I deserve to go through what You went through a thousand times.

In Your mercy and compassion, soften my heart so that I can understand what You did. Lead me to greater comprehension of why You did this, that I might glimpse an inkling of Your grace. On my own, I haven't been able to discover the depth of Your love for me.

Only You know the way into my heart and what is required to turn to You. Rather than trust that I am able to cover the stain of my sin with good deeds and religious rituals, guide me to pour the reservoir of my sin into Your wounds. Bring me the peace of knowing You loved me enough to willingly bear my punishment.

Now that sin's price is paid and the pain has been borne, I will watch in awe as the resurrection swallows and destroys my sin, along with the rest of the world's sin. O happy day! Grant me trust beyond doubt that all debt is satisfied and no sin remains. Faith like this can only come as a gift from You.

I declare sin and all wrongdoing to be my enemies. I want to live to please You and bring glory to God. The love and goodness I see in Your sacrifice for the world far exceeds all the power or wisdom I have attributed to Your Being. May the sufferings You experienced be the model for my life.

When trials cause me pain, let me remember the nails and thorns that pierced Your skin. When I, as Your follower, am pressured to do what I don't want to do, let me remember how You were led where You didn't want to go. When pride attacks me and calls me foolish for sacrificing myself for others, let me recall how You were mocked and disgraced. Take away any fear that makes me think following You will bring greater suffering than blessing. Teach me to incorporate Your life into my life, for You showed the way of eternal life. Amen.

4. Strange and dreadful was the fray,
   When Death and Life contended;
   But 'twas Life that won the day,
   And Death's dark sway was ended.
   Holy Scripture plainly saith,
   Death is swallowed up of Death,
   Put to scorn and led in triumph.
   Hallelujah!

5. This, the Paschal Lamb, the Christ,
   Whom God so freely gave us,
   On the cross is sacrificed
   In flames of love to save us.
   On our door the blood-mark:—Faith
   Holds it in the face of Death.
   The Destroyer can not harm us.
   Hallelujah!
   (Luther 1884b)

* * *

24. Now this is the fruit, that even as we have eaten and drunk the body and blood of Christ the Lord, we in turn permit ourselves to be eaten and drunk, and say the same words to our neighbor, Take, eat and drink; and this by no means in jest, but in all seriousness, meaning to offer yourself with all your life, even as Christ did with all that he had, in the sacramental words. (Vol. 2:208)

* * *

A Prayer for Confession and the Lord's Supper

Bread from Heaven,

I approach Your holy table with mixed feelings. I cannot fathom why You laid down Your life for me when I show so little effort in following Your will. I am ashamed that I have treated my neighbors poorly. I confess my weaknesses and my pitiful choices with a heavy heart, and I promise to work harder to be pleasing to You. Give me strength to lay down my pride and admit my wrongs to the ones I have offended, for in this, healing begins. Hearing the words "you are forgiven" is like soothing ointment in an open wound when I realize You, the Word, say this to me personally. Thank You, Jesus.

It seems like whenever I come to You, I'm always asking for something. I come to You now because I trust in You and I want the world to know I am committed to following You. Grant me courage and strength to exercise faith in a manner that reveals I am Your disciple. When I come to this holy meal thinking I am pure and pious because of anything I have done, do not look away in disgust. Gently humble me and bring me to my knees before You.

As I receive You in the bread and wine, remind me how You willingly gave Your body and blood to banish sin, death, hell, and sorrow from me. Comfort my spirit and free my mind so that sin is no longer my master. Surrounded in Your blessing and grace, empower me with a desire to bear the fruit of this meal—Christian love. Now I am Your body and Your blood to be offered to my neighbor.

Open my eyes to see where I can serve, or teach, or pray, or feed those who are in need. I want to follow Your example. Give me patience and tolerance as I work with people who are weak in faith and lacking in compassion. Give me the capacity to do this, not imagining I will be able to do it perfectly, but to the degree my shortcomings permit. Beloved of the Father, awaken me to understand that I must be intentional in my efforts to bear fruit in love. And when I don't see myself producing good fruits, draw me back to Your precious sacrament on my knees.

You are Love. When I receive You in the bread and wine, become the power of Love in me that shares You with my neighbor. Unite me with others in Your body that we may be woven together in our giving to each other. Comfort me and convict me in this life of faith. I want to grow and be strengthened. In Your transforming power, make me a new person, a servant capable of great love. Amen.

6. Therefore let us keep the feast
   With heartfelt exultation;
   God to shine on us is pleased,
   The Sun of our salvation.
   On our hearts, with heavenly grace,
   Beams the brightness of his face,
   And the night of sin has vanished.
   Hallelujah!

7. Eat th' unleavened bread to-day,
   And drink the paschal chalice;
   From God's pure word put away
   The leaven of guile and malice.
   Christ alone our souls will feed;
   He is meat and drink indeed.
   Faith no other life desireth.
   Hallelujah!
   (Luther 1884b)

Works Cited

Ambrose. 1884. "Saviour of the Heathen, Known." Translated from the Latin by Martin Luther. Translated from the German by Richard Massie. *The Hymns of Martin Luther.* Edited by Leonard Woolsey Bacon. London: Hodder and Stoughton. http://oll.libertyfund.org/754/.

Huss, John. 1884. "Christ, Who Freed Our Souls from Danger." Amended by Martin Luther. Translated by Richard Massie. *The Hymns of Martin Luther.* Edited by Leonard Woolsey Bacon. London: Hodder and Stoughton. http://oll.libertyfund.org/754/.

Luther, Martin. 1884a. "All Praise to Jesus' Hallowed Name." Translated chiefly by Richard Massie. *The Hymns of Martin Luther.* Edited by Leonard Woolsey Bacon. London: Hodder and Stoughton. http://oll.libertyfund.org/754/.

———. 1884b. "Christ was Laid in Death's Strong Bands." *The Hymns of Martin Luther.* Edited by Leonard Woolsey Bacon. London: Hodder and Stoughton. http://oll.libertyfund.org/754/.

———. 1884c. "Come, God Creator, Holy Ghost." *The Hymns of Martin Luther.* Edited by Leonard Woolsey Bacon. London: Hodder and Stoughton. http://oll.libertyfund.org/754/.

———. 1884d. "Come, Holy Spirit, Lord Our God." Translated by Arthur Tozer Russell. *The Hymns of Martin Luther.* Edited by Leonard Woolsey Bacon. London: Hodder and Stoughton. http://oll.libertyfund.org/754/.

———. 1884e. "Dear Christians, One and All Rejoice." Translated in part by Richard Massie. *The Hymns of Martin Luther.* Edited by Leonard Woolsey Bacon. London: Hodder and Stoughton. http://oll.libertyfund.org/754/.

———. 1884f. "From Heaven Above to Earth I Come." Translated by Catherine Winkworth (amended). *The Hymns of Martin Luther.* Edited by Leonard Woolsey Bacon. London: Hodder and Stoughton. http://oll.libertyfund.org/754/.

———. 1884g. "God, the Father, with Us Stay." Translated by Richard Massie. *The Hymns of Martin Luther.* Edited by Leonard Woolsey Bacon. London: Hodder and Stoughton. http://oll.libertyfund.org/754/.

———. 1884h. "Had God Not Come, May Israel Say." Translated by Richard Massie. *The Hymns of Martin Luther.* Edited by Leonard Woolsey Bacon. London: Hodder and Stoughton. http://oll.libertyfund.org/754/.

———. 1884i. "In Peace and Joy I Now Depart." *The Hymns of Martin Luther.* Edited by Leonard Woolsey Bacon. London: Hodder and Stoughton. http://oll.libertyfund.org/754/.

———. 1884j. "Jesus Christ, Who Came to Save." *The Hymns of Martin Luther.* Edited by Leonard Woolsey Bacon. London: Hodder and Stoughton. http://oll.libertyfund.org/754/.

———. 1884k. "Look Down, O Lord, from Heaven Behold." Translated by Frances Elizabeth Cox. *The Hymns of Martin Luther.* Edited by Leonard Woolsey Bacon. London: Hodder and Stoughton. http://oll.libertyfund.org/754/.

———. 1884l. "Lord God, Thy Praise We Sing" (modification of "Te Deum laudamus"). Translated by Richard Massie (amended). *The Hymns of Martin Luther.* Edited by Leonard Woolsey Bacon. London: Hodder and Stoughton. http://oll.libertyfund.org/754/.

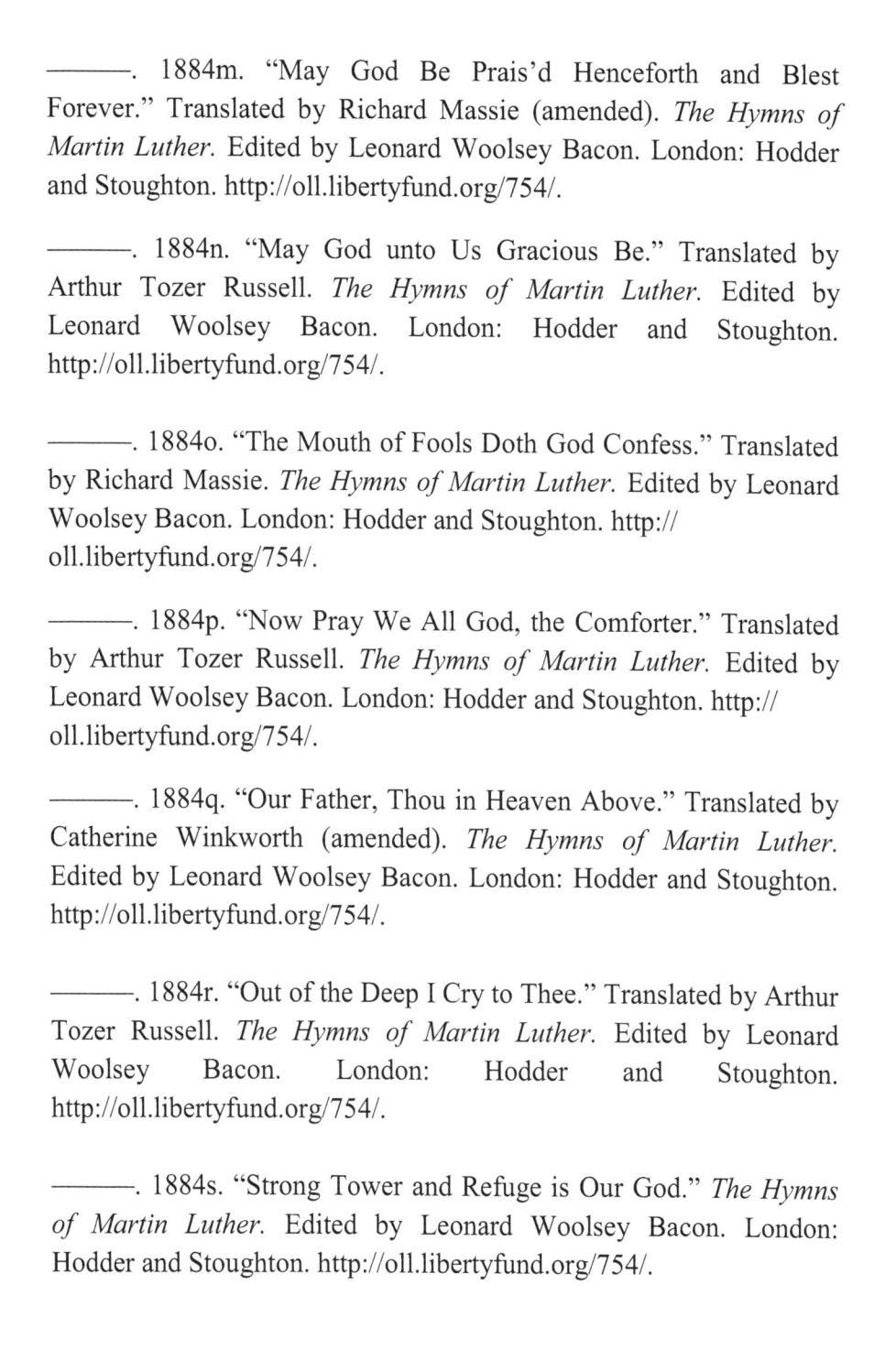

———. 1884m. "May God Be Prais'd Henceforth and Blest Forever." Translated by Richard Massie (amended). *The Hymns of Martin Luther*. Edited by Leonard Woolsey Bacon. London: Hodder and Stoughton. http://oll.libertyfund.org/754/.

———. 1884n. "May God unto Us Gracious Be." Translated by Arthur Tozer Russell. *The Hymns of Martin Luther*. Edited by Leonard Woolsey Bacon. London: Hodder and Stoughton. http://oll.libertyfund.org/754/.

———. 1884o. "The Mouth of Fools Doth God Confess." Translated by Richard Massie. *The Hymns of Martin Luther*. Edited by Leonard Woolsey Bacon. London: Hodder and Stoughton. http://oll.libertyfund.org/754/.

———. 1884p. "Now Pray We All God, the Comforter." Translated by Arthur Tozer Russell. *The Hymns of Martin Luther*. Edited by Leonard Woolsey Bacon. London: Hodder and Stoughton. http://oll.libertyfund.org/754/.

———. 1884q. "Our Father, Thou in Heaven Above." Translated by Catherine Winkworth (amended). *The Hymns of Martin Luther*. Edited by Leonard Woolsey Bacon. London: Hodder and Stoughton. http://oll.libertyfund.org/754/.

———. 1884r. "Out of the Deep I Cry to Thee." Translated by Arthur Tozer Russell. *The Hymns of Martin Luther*. Edited by Leonard Woolsey Bacon. London: Hodder and Stoughton. http://oll.libertyfund.org/754/.

———. 1884s. "Strong Tower and Refuge is Our God." *The Hymns of Martin Luther*. Edited by Leonard Woolsey Bacon. London: Hodder and Stoughton. http://oll.libertyfund.org/754/.

———. 1884t. "That Man a Godly Life Might Live." Translated by Richard Massie. *The Hymns of Martin Luther.* Edited by Leonard Woolsey Bacon. London: Hodder and Stoughton. http://oll.libertyfund.org/754/.

———. 1884u. "Though in Midst of Life We Be." Translated by Richard Massie. *The Hymns of Martin Luther.* Edited by Leonard Woolsey Bacon. London: Hodder and Stoughton. http://oll.libertyfund.org/754/.

———. 1884v. "To Jordan Came Our Lord the Christ." Translated by Richard Massie (amended). *The Hymns of Martin Luther.* Edited by Leonard Woolsey Bacon. London: Hodder and Stoughton. http://oll.libertyfund.org/754/.

———. 1884w. "To Shepherds, as They Watched by Night." Translated by Richard Massie. *The Hymns of Martin Luther.* Edited by Leonard Woolsey Bacon. London: Hodder and Stoughton. http://oll.libertyfund.org/754/.

———. 1884x. "We All Believe in One True God." *The Hymns of Martin Luther.* Edited by Leonard Woolsey Bacon. London: Hodder and Stoughton. http://oll.libertyfund.org/754/.

———. 1884y. "Why, Herod, Unrelenting Foe." Translated by Richard Massie. *The Hymns of Martin Luther.* Edited by Leonard Woolsey Bacon. London: Hodder and Stoughton. http://oll.libertyfund.org/754/.

———. 1884z. "Wilt Thou, O Man, Live Happily." Translated by Richard Massie (adapted). *The Hymns of Martin Luther.* Edited by Leonard Woolsey Bacon. London: Hodder and Stoughton. http://oll.libertyfund.org/754/.

———. 1956. *Luther's Works.* Vol. 21. Edited by Jaroslav Pelikan. St. Louis: Concordia Publishing House. 1955–1971.

———. 1983. *Sermons of Martin Luther*. Translated and edited by John Nicholas Lenker. Grand Rapids: Baker Book House.

About the author:

Paul W. Meier received a Masters of Divinity degree from Vanderbilt Divinity School and a Masters of Sacred Theology from Lutheran Theological Southern Seminary. He is a second career Lutheran pastor who has been published in The Upper Room, Christ In Our Home, Pray!, Alive Now, The Lutheran, and Lutheran Partners.

See other books by Paul W. Meier at
http://www.prayingthegospels.com/books

Made in the USA
Lexington, KY
04 October 2013